THE BLACKS

A Clown Show

JEAN GENET

Translated from the French by
BERNARD FRECHTMAN

FABER AND FABER

London

First published in 1960
by Faber and Faber Limited
24 Russell Square London W.C.1
First published in this edition 1967
Reprinted 1969
Printed in Great Britain by
Latimer Trend & Co Ltd Whitstable

SBN 571 08166 5

One evening an actor asked me to write a play for an all-black cast. But what exactly is a black? First of all, what's his colour?

J. G.

This play, written, I repeat, by a white man, is intended for a white audience, but if—which is unlikely—it is ever performed before a black audience, then a white person, male or female, should be invited every evening. The organizer of the show should welcome him formally, dress him in ceremonial costume and lead him to his seat, preferably in the front row of the stalls. The actors will play for him. A spotlight should be focused upon this symbolic white throughout the performance.

But what if no white person accepted? Then let white masks be distributed to the black spectators as they enter the theatre. And if the blacks refuse, then let a dummy be used.

J. G.

All enquiries regarding performing rights should be addressed to:
Mrs. Rosica Colin, 4 Hereford Square, London, S.W.7.

*

LES NÈGRES was first performed by La Compagnie Africaine d'Art Dramatique 'Les Griots' at the Théâtre de Lutèce, Paris, on 28th October 1959. It was directed by Roger Blin, with décor by André Acquart and choreography by Edée Fortin. The cast was as follows:

NEWPORT NEWS	*Robert Liensol*
BOBO	*Toto Bissainthe*
VIRTUE	*Lydia Ewande*
VILLAGE	*Bachir Touré*
FELICITY	*Darling Legitimus*
ARCHIBALD	*Mamadou Condé*
DIOUF	*Gérard Lemoine*
SNOW	*Judith Aucagos*
THE JUDGE	*Dia Fara*
THE QUEEN	*Gisèle Baka*
THE VALET	*Edée Fortin*
THE MISSIONARY	*Georges Hilarion*
THE GOVERNOR GENERAL	*Théo Legitimus*

7

THE BLACKS

*

The curtain is drawn. Not raised—drawn.

THE SET. *Black velvet curtains. Right and left, a few sets of tiers with landings of different heights. One of them, far in the background, toward the right, is higher than the others. Another, rather like a gallery, goes up to the flies and all around the stage. That is where the Court will appear. A green screen is set on a higher landing, just a trifle lower than the one mentioned above. In the middle of the stage, on the floor, a catafalque, covered with a white cloth. On the catafalque, bouquets of flowers: irises, roses, gladioli, arum lilies. At the foot of the catafalque, a shoe-shine box. The lighting: very garish neon light.*

When the curtain is drawn, four negroes in evening clothes—no, one of them, NEWPORT NEWS, *who is barefoot, is wearing a woollen sweater—and four negresses in evening gowns are dancing a kind of minuet around the catafalque to an air of Mozart which they whistle and hum. The evening clothes—white ties for the gentlemen—are accompanied by tan shoes. The ladies' costumes—heavily spangled evening gowns—suggest fake elegance, the very height of bad taste. As they dance and whistle, they pluck flowers from their bodices and lapels and lay them on the catafalque. Suddenly, on the high platform, left, enters the Court.*

THE COURT. *Each actor playing a member of the Court is a masked negro whose mask represents the face of a white person. The mask is worn in such a way that the audience sees a wide black band all around it, and even the actor's kinky hair.*

THE QUEEN. *White, sad mask. Drooping mouth. Royal crown on her head. Sceptre in her hand. Ermine-trimmed cloak with a train. Superb gown. At her right:*

HER VALET. *A puny, mincing little fellow wearing a valet's striped waistcoat. On his arm a towel, with which he toys as if it were a scarf, but with which he will wipe Her Majesty's eyes.*

9

THE GOVERNOR. *Sublime uniform. Is holding a pair of field-glasses.*

THE JUDGE. *Black and red robe. At the Queen's left.*

THE MISSIONARY. *White robe. Rings. Pectoral cross. At the Judge's left.*

The members of the Court, all standing on the same tier, seem interested in the spectacle of the dancing Negroes, who suddenly stop short, breaking off the minuet. The Negroes approach the footlights, make a ninety-degree turn, and bow ceremoniously to the Court,[1] then to the audience. One of them steps forth and speaks, addressing now the audience, now the Court:

ARCHIBALD: Ladies and gentlemen. . . . (*The Court bursts into very shrill, but very well-orchestrated laughter. It is not free and easy laughter. This laughter is echoed by the same but even shriller laughter of the Negroes who are standing about Archibald. The Court, bewildered, becomes silent.*) . . . My name is Archibald Absalom Wellington. (*He bows, then moves from one to the other, naming each in turn.*) . . . This is Mr. Deodatus Village (*he bows*) . . . Miss Adelaide Bobo (*she bows*) . . . Mr. Edgar Alas Newport News (*he bows*) . . . Mrs. Augustus Snow (*she remains upright*) . . . well . . . well . . . madame (*roaring angrily*) bow! (*she remains upright*) . . . I'm asking you, madame, to bow! (*extremely gentle, almost grieved*) I'm asking you, madame, to bow—it's a performance. (SNOW *bows*) . . . Mrs. Felicity Trollop Pardon (*she bows*) . . . and Miss Diop—Stephanie Virtue Secret-rose Diop.

DIOUF: And me.

ARCHIBALD: And he.—As you see, ladies and gentlemen, just as you have your lilies and roses, so we—in order to serve you—shall use our beautiful,

[1] In Roger Blin's production, the Court entered from the auditorium, after the curtain had been drawn. (Author's note)

shiny-black make-up. It is Mr. Deodatus
Village who gathers the smoke-black and Mrs.
Felicity Trollop Pardon who thins it out in our
saliva. These ladies help her. We embellish
ourselves so as to please you. You are White.
And spectators. This evening we shall perform
for you. . . .

THE QUEEN: (*interrupting the speaker*). Bishop! Bishop-at-
large!

THE MISSIONARY: (*leaning toward her, though without changing
place*). Hallelujah!

THE QUEEN: (*plaintively*). Are they going to kill her?

(*The* NEGROES *below burst into the same shrill
and orchestrated laughter as before. But*
ARCHIBALD *silences them.*)

ARCHIBALD: Be quiet. If all they have is their nostalgia, let
them enjoy it.

SNOW: Grief, sir, is another of their adornments. . . .

THE VALET: (*looking about him*). What's happened to my
chair?

THE MISSIONARY: (*doing the same*). And to mine? Who took it?

THE VALET: (*to* THE MISSIONARY, *querulously*). If my chair
hadn't disappeared too, you'd have suspected
me. It was my turn to sit down, but I don't
know where the hell my chair is. You can count
on my good humour and devotion if I have to
remain standing all through the show.

THE QUEEN: (*increasingly languid*). I repeat—are they going
to kill her?

THE MISSIONARY: (*very sombrely*). But Madame . . . (*a pause*)
she's dead!

11

THE VALET: Is that all you can say to your sovereign? (*As if to himself.*) This crowd could stand a good clouting.

THE MISSIONARY: The poor unfortunate has been in my prayers since this morning. In the very forefront.

THE QUEEN: (*leaning forward to call* SNOW). Is it true, young lady, that all we have left is our sadness and that it's one of our adornments?

ARCHIBALD: And we haven't finished embellishing you. This evening we've come again to round out your grief.

THE GOVERNOR: (*shaking his fist and making as if to descend*). If I let you!

THE VALET: (*holding him back*). Where are you going?

THE GOVERNOR: (*with a martial air*). To stamp out the Blacks!

(*The* NEGROES *below shrug their shoulders in unison.*)

ARCHIBALD: Be quiet. (*To the audience.*) This evening we shall perform for you. But, in order that you may remain comfortably settled in your seats in the presence of the drama that is already unfolding here, in order that you be assured that there is no danger of such a drama's worming its way into your precious lives, we shall even have the decency—a decency learned from you—to make communication impossible. We shall increase the distance that separates us —a distance that is basic—by our pomp, our manners, our insolence—for we are also actors. When my speech is over, everything here—(*he stamps his foot in a gesture of rage*) here!—will take place in the delicate world of reprobation. If we sever bonds, may a continent drift off and may Africa sink or fly away. . . .

12

(*For some moments,* THE GOVERNOR, *who had taken a paper from his pocket, has been reading in a low voice.*)

THE QUEEN: May it fly away—was that a metaphor?

THE GOVERNOR: (*reading more and more loudly*). ". . . when I fall to earth, scurvily pierced by your spears, look closely, you will behold my ascension. (*In a thundering voice.*) My corpse will be on the ground, but my soul and body will rise into the air. . . ."

THE VALET: (*shrugging his shoulders*). Learn your role backstage. As for that last sentence, it oughtn't to be rolled out as if it were a proclamation.

THE GOVERNOR: (*turning to* THE VALET). I know what I'm doing. (*He resumes his reading.*) "You'll see them and you'll die of fright. First, you'll turn pale, and then you'll fall, and you'll be dead. . . ." (*He folds the paper and puts it back into his pocket very conspicuously.*) That was a device to let them know that we know. And we know that we've come to attend our own funeral rites. They think they're compelling us, but it is owing to our good breeding that we shall descend to death. Our suicide. . . .

THE QUEEN: (*touching* THE GOVERNOR *with her fan*). . . . Preparations for it have begun, but let the negro speak. Look at that poor, gaping mouth of his, and those columns of flies streaming out of it . . . (*she looks more closely, leaning forward*) . . . or swarming into it. (*To* ARCHIBALD.) Continue.

ARCHIBALD: (*after bowing to* THE QUEEN). . . .sink or fly away. (*The members of the Court protect their faces, as if a bird were flying at them.*) . . . but let it be off! (*A pause.*) When we leave this

13

stage, we are involved in your life. I am a cook, this lady is a sewing-maid, this gentleman is a medical student, this gentleman is a curate at St. Anne's, this lady . . . skip it. Tonight, our sole concern will be to entertain you. So we have killed this white woman. There she lies. (*He points to the catafalque. The members of the Court wipe away a tear with a very theatrical gesture and heave a long sob of grief to which the* NEGROES *respond with their very shrill and perfectly orchestrated laughter.*) . . . Only *we* could have done it the way we did it— savagely. And now, listen . . . (*He takes a step back.*) . . . listen . . . oh, I was forgetting, thieves that we are, we have tried to filch your fine language. Liars that we are, the names I have mentioned to you are false. Listen . . . (*He steps back, but the other actors have stopped listening to him.* MRS. FELICITY, *an imposing sixty-year-old negress, has gone up to the top tier, right, where she sits down in an armchair, facing the Court.*)

BOBO: The flowers, the flowers! Don't touch them!

SNOW: (*taking an iris for her bodice*). Are they yours, or the murdered woman's?

BOBO: They're there for the performance. Which doesn't require that you burst into bloom. Put back the iris. Or the rose. Or the tulip.

ARCHIBALD: Bobo's right. You wanted to be more attractive —there's some blacking left.

SNOW: All right. Although. . . . (*She spits out the flower after biting into it.*)

ARCHIBALD: No needless cruelty, Snow. And no garbage here.

(SNOW *picks up the flower and eats it.* ARCHIBALD

14

runs after SNOW, *who hides behind the catafalque.*
VILLAGE *catches her and brings her back to*
ARCHIBALD, *who wants to lecture her.*)

SNOW: (*to* VILLAGE). A regular cop!

ARCHIBALD: (*to* SNOW). The rite doesn't call for your
behaving like a spoiled child. (*While all the
other* NEGROES *stand still and listen, he turns to*
NEWPORT NEWS.) And you, sir, you're
superfluous. As everything is secret, you've got
to get going. Clear out. Go tell them. Let them
know we've started. They're to do their job,
just as we'll do ours. Everything will go off in
the usual way. I hope so.

(NEWPORT NEWS *bows and is about to leave by
the left wing, but* VILLAGE *stops him.*)

VILLAGE: Not that way, you fool. You were told not to
come back. You're spoiling everything.

NEWPORT NEWS: The trouble. . . .

ARCHIBALD: (*interrupting him*). Later. Get going.

(*Exit* NEWPORT NEWS, *left.*)

SNOW: (*spitting out the iris*). You always start by
picking on me.

BOBO: You let your moods get the better of you. You
give way to your temperament, and you've no
right to.

SNOW: I have! Because of my special outlook on the
whole business. If it weren't for me. . . .

ARCHIBALD: You've done neither more nor less than the
others.

SNOW: And my moods are special too, and so is my
temperament, and they suit your purpose. And
if it weren't for my jealousy where you're
concerned, Village. . . .

15

VILLAGE: (*interrupting her*). We know all about it. You've repeated it often enough. Long before her death (*pointing to the catafalque*) you hated her bitterly. But her death wasn't meant to signify merely that she lost her life. With tenderness we all brooded over it, but not lovingly. (*A long sob from the Court.*)

SNOW: Really? Then let me tell you now—all of you— I've been burning for so long, burning with such ardent hatred, that I'm a heap of ashes.

DIOUF: What about us? What are we?

SNOW: It's not the same thing, gentlemen. There was a touch of desire in your hatred of her, which means a touch of love. But I, and they (*pointing to the other women*), we, the negresses, we had only our wrath and rage. When she was killed, we felt no awe, no fear, but no tenderness either. We were dry, gentlemen. Dry, like the breasts of old Bambara women.

(THE QUEEN *bursts out laughing.* THE MISSIONARY *motions to her to be quiet. Holding her handkerchief to her mouth,* THE QUEEN *gradually calms down.*)

ARCHIBALD: (*severely*). The tragedy will lie in the colour black! It's *that* that you'll cherish, *that* that you'll attain, and deserve. It's *that* that must be earned.

SNOW: (*ecstatically*). My colour! Why, you're my very self! But you, Village, what was it you wanted in going after her? (*She points to the catafalque.*)

VILLAGE: You're starting again with your silly suspicions. Do you want a detailed description of the humiliations she made me feel? Do you? Tell me, do you?

16

ALL: (*with a terrible cry*). Yes!

VILLAGE: Negroes, you've yelled too soon and too loud. (*He takes a deep breath.*) This evening, there'll be something new.

ARCHIBALD: You've no right to change anything in the ceremonial, unless, of course, you hit upon some cruel detail that heightens it.

VILLAGE: In any case, I can keep you on tenterhooks waiting for the murder.

ARCHIBALD: You're to obey *me*. And the text we've prepared.

VILLAGE: (*banteringly*). But I'm still free to speed up or draw out my recital and my performance. I can move in slow motion, can't I? I can sigh more often and more deeply.

THE QUEEN: (*amused*). He's charming! Continue, young man!

THE JUDGE: Indeed, your Majesty is forgetting herself!

THE VALET: I rather like him, I must say. (*To* VILLAGE.) Do sigh more often and more deeply, charming blackboy!

THE GOVERNOR: (*to* THE VALET). That'll do! Instead of that, tell us how rubber stands on the stock-exchange.

THE VALET: (*saluting, and in a single breath*). Goodyear, 4,500. (*The members of the Court pull a long face.*)

THE GOVERNOR: What about gold?

THE VALET: Eastern Ubangi 1,580 Saint Johnny-get-your-gun 1,050. Macupia 2,002. M'Zaita 20,008.

(*The Members of the Court rub their hands.*)

VILLAGE: (*continuing*). . . . can sigh more often and more deeply, can relax in the middle of a sentence or

17

word. Besides, I'm tired. You forget that I'm already knocked out from the crime I had to finish off before you arrived, since you need a fresh corpse for every performance.

THE QUEEN: (*with a cry*). Oh!

THE JUDGE: (*fiercely*). I told you so.

THE VALET: (*very affectedly*). Don't condemn them at the very start. Listen to them. They're exquisitely spontaneous. They have a strange beauty. Their flesh is weightier. . . .

THE GOVERNOR: Be quiet, you whippersnapper! You and your damned exoticism!

DIOUF: (*to* ARCHIBALD). Actually, we *could* use the same corpse a number of times. Its presence is the thing that counts.

ARCHIBALD: What about the smell, Mr. Vicar General?

BOBO: (*to* ARCHIBALD). Does the stench frighten you now? That's what rises from my African soil. I, Bobo, want to draw my train over its thick waves! May I be wafted up by a smell of carrion! And carried off! (*To the Court.*) And you, pale and odourless race, race without animal odours, without the pestilence of our swamps. . . .

ARCHIBALD: (*to* BOBO). Let Virtue speak.

VIRTUE: (*prudently*). All the same, we ought to be careful. It gets more dangerous every day. Not only for Village, but for every hunter.

SNOW: All the better. Since we're working this evening for a Court of Justice that's been set up especially for us, we'll dedicate our follies to it.

ARCHIBALD: That'll do. (*To* VILLAGE.) Tell me, Village, there

18

wasn't any alert this evening either, was there? Everything went off smoothly, I hope. Where did you find her?

VILLAGE: I told you just before, when I arrived. Right after dinner, Mr. Herod Adventure and I were walking along the docks. The evening was rather mild. A little before the entrance to the bridge, there was an old tramp squatting—or lying—on a pile of rags. But I've told you all about it. . . .

BOBO: The old tramp may consider herself fortunate. She'll have a first-class funeral.

ARCHIBALD: (*to* VILLAGE). But tell us more. Did she scream?

VILLAGE: Not at all. Hadn't time to. Mr. Herod Adventure and I went straight up to her. She was dozing. She half awoke. The blackness of the night. . . .

BOBO & SNOW: (*laughing*). Oh! the blackness!

VILLAGE: In the darkness, she must have taken us for policemen. She reeked of drink, like all the others thrown out on the docks. She said, "I'm not doing any harm. . . ."

ARCHIBALD: And then?

VILLAGE: As usual. It was I who bent down. Mr. Herod Adventure held her hands while I strangled her. She stiffened a bit . . . then she had what's called a spasm, and that was that. Mr. Herod Adventure was slightly nauseated by the crone's face, by the smell of drink and urine, by the filth. He almost puked. But he pulled himself together. We carried her to our Cadillac and brought her here, in a crate.

(*A pause.*)

SNOW: But that stench, which isn't ours. . . .

(VILLAGE *takes a cigarette from his pocket.*)

BOBO: You're right, let's smoke.

(*The* NEGROES *seem not quite to understand.*)

ARCHIBALD: Let's all have a cigarette. Let's smoke her out.

(*Each* NEGRO *takes a cigarette from his pocket. They light matches for each other, bowing ceremoniously as they do, then arrange themselves in a circle and puff smoke around the catafalque. With their mouths closed, they hum a kind of sing-song that begins: "I liked my white sheep . . .")*
(*During the sing-song the Court grows agitated.*)

THE GOVERNOR: (*to the* VALET). Now they're smoking her out! It's a hive, it's a nest of hornets, it's a wooden bed swarming with bed-bugs, it's a burrow, it's a den of rebels. . . . Our corpse! They're going to cook her and eat her! Take their matches away!

(*The entire Court kneels before* THE QUEEN; THE VALET *dries her eyes with a towel.*)

THE MISSIONARY: Let us pray, Madame. (*To the others.*) All of you, on your knees before that august grief.

THE QUEEN: Ahaaha!

THE MISSIONARY: Have confidence, your Majesty, God is white.

THE VALET: You seem sure of yourself. . . .

THE MISSIONARY: Would he have allowed—you young milksop— would he have allowed the Miracle of Greece? For two thousand years God has been white. He eats from a white tablecloth. He wipes his white mouth with a white napkin. He picks at white meat with a white fork. (*A pause.*) He watches the snow fall.

20

ARCHIBALD: (*to* VILLAGE). Recite the rest to them. Any trouble on the way back?

VILLAGE: None at all. Besides, I had this. (*After working the breech noisily, he shows a revolver, which he lays on the shoeshine box, where it will remain.*)

VIRTUE: (*still very calm*). But after all, do you imagine that this kind of thing can go on much longer, these corpses that are discovered at dawn—and even in broad daylight—in disgusting places and postures? Sooner or later there'll be a big blow-up. And we've got to beware of possible betrayal.

SNOW: What do you mean?

VIRTUE: That a negro is capable of ratting on another negro.

SNOW: Speak for yourself, madame.

VIRTUE: It's because of what I see and what goes on in my own soul and what I call the temptation of the Whites. . . .

THE GOVERNOR: (*triumphantly*). I was sure of it. Sooner or later, they come round. All you have to do is pay the price.

THE QUEEN: I'll offer my jewels! I have cellars full of chests full of pearls fished up by them from their mysterious seas, diamonds, gold, pieces of eight unearthed from their deep mines, I'll give them away, throw them away. . . .

THE VALET: What about me?

THE QUEEN: You'll still have your queen, you naughty boy. . . . Aged, in rags, but stately. Grand.

ARCHIBALD: (*to* THE QUEEN). Allow us to continue.

THE JUDGE: (*to* ARCHIBALD). It's you who keep stalling. You

21

promised us a re-enactment of the crime so as to deserve your condemnation. The Queen's waiting. Hurry up.

ARCHIBALD: (*to* THE JUDGE). No one's co-operating. Except Virtue.

THE JUDGE: Well then, let Virtue lead off, or Village.

VILLAGE: (*panicky*). Negroes, it's not time yet for the part to be declaimed. All I have to say now is that the woman was white and that she gave our smell as an excuse for running away. For running away, because she didn't dare chase me. Ah, the great days when they used to hunt the negro and the antelope! My father once told me. . . .

ARCHIBALD: (*interrupting him*). Your father? Sir, don't use that word again! There was a shade of tenderness in your voice as you uttered it.

VILLAGE: And what do you suggest I call the male who knocked up the negress who gave birth to me?

ARCHIBALD: Dammit, do the best you can. Invent—if not words, then phrases that cut you off rather than bind you. Invent not love but hatred, and thereby make poetry, since that's the only domain in which we're allowed to operate. For their entertainment? (*Pointing to the audience.*) We'll see. You referred, quite rightly, to our smell—our scent, which used to lead their hounds to us in the bush—you were on the right track. Take a whiff and say that "she" (*pointing to the catafalque*) knew that we stink. Proceed delicately. Be clever and choose only reasons for hatred. Keep from magnifying our savageness. Be careful not to seem a wild beast. If you do, you'll tempt their desire without gaining their esteem. So you murdered her.

22

We're going to begin. . . .

VILLAGE: Just a minute. What can I substitute for the word father?

ARCHIBALD: Your circumlocution is quite satisfactory.

VILLAGE: It's rather long.

ARCHIBALD: By stretching language, we'll distort it sufficiently to wrap ourselves in it and hide, whereas the masters contract it.

BOBO: Generally I'm brief.

ARCHIBALD: You're generally eager to see the others hide behind their words. But, like us, my dear Bobo, you delight the ear with morning-glories that twine round the pillars of the world. We must charm. From their toes to their ears, our pink tongues—the only part of us that suggests a flower—move artfully and silently round and about our fine, lackadaisical ladies and gentlemen. Will the phrase do?

VILLAGE: Yours?

ARCHIBALD: Yours, stupid . . . "the negro who knocked up" and so on. . . . Does everyone approve? Except Snow—still stubborn?

SNOW: (*very acrimoniously*). If I were sure that Village bumped the woman off in order to heighten the fact that he's a scarred, smelly, thick-lipped, snub-nosed negro, an eater and guzzler of Whites and all other colours, a drooling, sweating, belching, spitting, coughing, farting goat-f——r, a licker of white boots, a good-for-nothing, sick, oozing oil and sweat, limp and submissive, if I were sure he killed her in order to merge with the night. . . . But I know he loved her.

23

VIRTUE: He didn't.

VILLAGE: I didn't.

SNOW: (*to* VIRTUE). So you think he loves you, you, the submissive negress?

ARCHIBALD: (*severely*). Snow!

SNOW: (*to* VIRTUE). To turn pink, to blush with emotion, with confusion—tender expressions that will never apply to us. Otherwise you'd see Virtue's cheeks turn flaming purple.

VIRTUE: Mine?

BOBO: Someone's.

(*All the* NEGROES *are now gathered at the right. They cease to speak.* NEWPORT NEWS *enters from the wings. He moves forward quietly.*)

ARCHIBALD: (*going up to him*). Well? Has anything happened yet?

NEWPORT NEWS: He's arrived. We've brought him along, handcuffed.

(*All the* NEGROES *cluster round* NEWPORT NEWS.)

SNOW: What are you going to do?

NEWPORT NEWS: (*bending down and picking up the revolver from the shoeshine box*). First of all, question him. . . .

ARCHIBALD: (*interrupting*). Say only what you have to. We're being watched.

(*They all look up at the Court.*)

THE JUDGE: (*crying out*). Just because you're disguised as trained dogs you think you know how to talk, and you start inventing riddles. . . .

VILLAGE: (*to* THE JUDGE). Some day. . . .

24

ARCHIBALD: (*interrupting*). Cut it out. If you lose your temper, you'll betray yourself and betray us. (*To* NEWPORT NEWS.) Did he say anything to justify himself? Anything at all?

NEWPORT NEWS: Nothing. Shall I go?

ARCHIBALD: When the Court of Justice has been set up, come back and let us know.

(NEWPORT NEWS *moves away from the group and is about to leave.*)

DIOUF: (*timidly*). Do you really want to take that object with you? (*Pointing to the revolver in* NEWPORT NEWS'S *hand.*)

ARCHIBALD: (*to* DIOUF, *violently*). I repeat once again—you're wasting your time. We know your argument. You're going to urge us to be reasonable, to be conciliatory. But we're bent on being hostile. You'll speak of love. Go right ahead, since our speeches are set down in the script. (*All except* DIOUF *and* NEWPORT NEWS *let out an orchestrated laugh.*)

NEWPORT NEWS: You really ought to listen to him. . . .

ARCHIBALD: (*imperiously*). Clear out! Get back into the wings. Take the revolver and go and do your job.

NEWPORT NEWS: But. . . .

VILLAGE: (*breaking in*). No buts about it. Obey Mr. Wellington. (*Resignedly*, NEWPORT NEWS *starts to leave, but* VILLAGE *stops him.*) Not that way, you fool! (*Exit* NEWPORT NEWS, *left.*)

BOBO: You asked for the floor, Mr. Clergyman. Speak up!

DIOUF: (*with an effort*). Everything about me seems ludicrous to you. I know it does. . . .

25

ARCHIBALD: Bear one thing in mind: we must deserve their reprobation and get them to deliver the judgement that will condemn us. I repeat, they know about our crime. . . .

DIOUF: All the same, let me try to come to an understanding with them, to propose some kind of agreement. . . .

ARCHIBALD: (*irritably*). All right, you may speak, Mr. Diouf. But we'll close our eyes and seal our mouths, and our empty faces will suggest the desert. Let's all shut up. . . .

DIOUF: (*panicky*). Gentlemen, gentlemen, ladies, don't leave!

ARCHIBALD: (*implacably*). Let's shut up! Let's efface ourselves. Now speak.

DIOUF: But who'll hear me? (*The Court burst out laughing.*) You? That's not possible. (*He wants to talk to the Negroes, but they have closed their eyes and mouths and put their hands over their ears.*) After all, gentlemen, my good friends, it's not a fresh corpse that we need. I'd like the ceremony to involve us, not in hatred. . . .

THE NEGROES: (*ironically, and in a dismal voice*). . . . but in love!

DIOUF: If it's possible, ladies and gentlemen.

THE MISSIONARY: . . . to involve you, above all, in your love of us.

THE VALET: Are you speaking seriously, monsignor?

THE JUDGE: Then we shall deign to hear you.

THE GOVERNOR: Although, after this orgy. . . .

DIOUF: (*with an appeasing gesture of his hand*). May I explain? I should indeed like the performance

26

to re-establish in our souls a balance that our plight perpetuates, but I should like it to unfold so harmoniously that they (*pointing to the audience*) see only the beauty of it, and I would like them to recognize us in that beauty which disposes them to love.

(*A long silence.*)

BOBO: (*slowly opening her eyes*). The crossing of the desert was long and arduous. Poor Diouf, finding no oasis, you probably opened your veins to drink a little blood!

THE MISSIONARY: (*after coughing*). Tell me, my dear Vicar, what about the host? Yes, the host. Will you invent a black host? And what will it be made of? Gingerbread, you say? That's brown.

DIOUF: But Monsignor, we have a thousand ingredients. We'll dye it. A grey host. . . .

THE GOVERNOR: (*breaking in*). Grant the grey host and you're sunk. You'll see—he'll demand further concessions, more oddities.

DIOUF: (*plaintively*). White on one side, black on the other?

THE VALET: (*to* DIOUF). Would you be so kind as to inform me—for, after all, I have chosen to be understanding—where the negro went with his revolver just before?

ARCHIBALD: Backstage. (*To* DIOUF.) And stop jabbering. Good God, anybody would think you were trying to make fun of us.

DIOUF: (*to* ARCHIBALD). Sir, I apologize. I'd like to glorify my colour, just as you do. The kindness of the whites settled upon my head, as it did upon yours. Though it rested there lightly, it was unbearable. Their intelligence descended on my right shoulder, and a whole flock of virtues on my left. And at times, when I opened my hands, I would find their charity nestling there. In my negro solitude, I feel the need, just as you do, to glorify my exquisite savageness, but I'm old and I think. . . .

BOBO: Who's asking you to? What we need is hatred. Our ideas will spring from hatred.

DIOUF: (*ironically*). You're a technician, Bobo, but it's not easy to cast off a guilty meekness that the heart desires. I've suffered too much shame not to want to befoul their beauteous souls, but. . . .

ARCHIBALD: No buts about it, or get out! My anger isn't make-believe.

DIOUF: Please, Archy. . . .

ARCHIBALD: Don't be so familiar. Not here. Politeness must be raised to such a pitch that it becomes monstrous. It must arouse fear. We're being observed by spectators. Sir, if you have any intention of presenting even the most trivial of their ideas without caricaturing it, then get out! Beat it!

BOBO: He wouldn't mind—it's his day off.

VILLAGE: Let him keep talking. The sound of his voice moves me.

SNOW: Bravo! I was expecting something like that from you. Because you, too, fear this moment. Perhaps because the action will separate you and Virtue for a while.

THE GOVERNOR: (*suddenly*). You were told what to do—start off with Village, start off with Virtue.

(*The* NEGROES *are taken aback for a moment and look at each other, then resign themselves.*)

28

VILLAGE: (*bowing to* VIRTUE, *and sighing deeply*). Madame, I bring you nothing comparable to what is called love. What is happening within me is very mysterious and cannot be accounted for by my colour. When I beheld you. . . .

ARCHIBALD: Be careful, Village, don't start referring to your real life.[1]

VILLAGE: (*with one knee on the floor*). When I beheld you, you were walking in the rain, in high heels. You were wearing a black silk dress, black stockings, patent-leather pumps and were carrying a black umbrella. Oh, if only I hadn't been born into slavery! I'd have been flooded with a strange emotion, but we—you and I— were moving along the edges of the world, out of bounds. We were the shadow, or the dark interior, of luminous creatures. . . . When I beheld you, suddenly—for perhaps a second— I had the strength to reject everything that wasn't you, and to laugh at the illusion. But my shoulders are very frail. I was unable to bear the weight of the world's condemnation. And I began to hate you when everything about you would have kindled my love and when love would have made men's contempt unbearable, and their contempt would have made my love unbearable. The fact is, I hate you.
(*For some moments, the Court seems to have been growing agitated.* THE VALET *seems to be yelling silently into the cupped ear of* THE GOVERNOR.)

ARCHIBALD: (*to the Court*). Please!

THE VALET: (*yelling*). M'Ziata 2,010!

[1] From this point until he says "Careful, Village," Archibald will saw the air with his hands like an orchestra leader, as if he were directing Village's recital. (Author's note)

THE GOVERNOR: What about coffee?

THE VALET: (*the entire Court listens very attentively*).
Extra-Special Arabica 608–627. Robusta
327–327. Kuilu 313–317.

VILLAGE: (*who had lowered his head, raises it to resume
his speech*). . . . I know not whether you are
beautiful. I fear you may be. I fear your
sparkling darkness. Oh darkness, stately mother
of my race, shadow, sheath that swathes me
from top to toe, long sleep in which the frailest
of your children would love to be shrouded, I
know not whether you are beautiful, but you
are Africa, oh monumental night, and I hate
you. I hate you for filling my black eyes with
sweetness. I hate you for making me thrust you
from me, for making me hate you. It would
take so little for your face, your body, your
movements, your heart to thrill me. . . .

ARCHIBALD: Careful, Village!

VILLAGE: (*to* VIRTUE). But I hate you! (*To the others.*) But
let me tell her and tell you about all the pain I
have to endure. If love is denied us, I want you
to know. . . .

BOBO: We know all about it. We're black too. But in
order to refer to ourselves, we don't adorn our
metaphors with stars. Or grand nocturnal
images. But with soot and blacking, with coal
and tar.

DIOUF: Don't make it so hard for him. If his suffering is
too intense, let him use language to ease the
strain.

VILLAGE: Ease the strain? I remember how I suffered to
see that tall gleaming body walking in the rain.
Her feet were getting soaked. . . .

30

BOBO: Her black feet. *Black* feet!

VILLAGE: In the rain. Virtue was walking in the rain, looking for White customers, as you know. No, no, there'll be no love for us. . . . (*He hesitates.*)

VIRTUE: You may speak. Every brothel has its negress.

THE GOVERNOR: (*after clearing his throat*). To the whorehouse, dammit! Egad, to the whorehouse! I make my troops tear off a piece every Saturday. Pox and chancres, doesn't matter a damn! Troops should end up lame and limping. To the whorehouse, dammit!

(*The entire Court applauds.* THE GOVERNOR *puffs himself up.*)

VIRTUE: Then let me tell you that this evening's ceremony will affect me less than the one I perform ten times a day. I'm the only one who experiences shame to the bitter end. . . .

ARCHIBALD: Don't allude to your life.

VIRTUE: (*ironically*). You've been infected by the squeamishness you've picked up from the Whites. A whore shocks you.

BOBO: She does, if she's one in real life. There's no need for us to know about your personal sufferings and dislikes. That's *your* business . . . in your room.

VILLAGE: This ceremony is painful to me.

ARCHIBALD: To us, too. They tell us that we're grown-up children. In that case, what's left for us? The theatre! We'll play at being reflected in it, and we'll see ourselves—big black narcissists—slowly disappearing into its waters.

VILLAGE: I don't want to disappear.

31

ARCHIBALD: You're no exception! Nothing will remain of you but the foam of your rage. Since they merge us with an image and drown us in it, let the image set their teeth on edge!

VILLAGE: My body wants to live.

ARCHIBALD: You're becoming a spectre before their very eyes and you're going to haunt them.

VILLAGE: I love Virtue. She loves me.

ARCHIBALD: Yes, she, perhaps. She has powers that you haven't. There are times when she dominates the Whites—oh, I know, by her magic wiggle. But that's also a way of dominating them. She can therefore bring you what most resembles love: tenderness. In her arms, you'll be her child, not her lover.

VILLAGE: (*obstinately*). I love Virtue.

ARCHIBALD: You think you love her. You're a negro and a performer. Neither of whom will know love. Now, this evening—but this evening only—we cease to be performers, since we are negroes. On this stage, we're like guilty prisoners who play at being guilty.

VILLAGE: We don't want to be guilty of anything any more. Virtue will be my wife.

ARCHIBALD: Then get the hell out of here. Beat it! Go away. Take her with you. Go join them (*pointing to the audience*) . . . if they'll have you. If they accept you both. And if you succeed in winning their love, come back and let me know. But first discolour yourselves. Get the hell out. Go join them. Go down and be spectators. *We'll* be saved by *that* (*pointing to the catafalque*).

THE VALET: (*in an oily tone*). Gentlemen, what if it

32

happened to be a man that you caught in your net one fine summer evening? What would you do about the seduction scene? Have you ever captured a carpenter with his plane? Or a bargeman with his canal-boats and his clothes hanging on a line?

BOBO: (*very insolently*). Yes, we have! We picked up an old down-and-out vaudeville singer: wrapped up and cased. There (*pointing to the catafalque*). Only too happy to dress him up for the ceremony as a governor-general, when he was killed before the eyes of the crowd—last night's, ladies and gentlemen. We deposited him in the attic. Where he still is (*pointing to the corpse*). Similarly, we did away with a decent, helpless old lady, a milkman, a postman, a seamstress, a government clerk. . . . (*The Court shrinks in horror.*)

THE VALET: (*persisting*). And what if there'd been nothing available but a four-year-old boy on his way home from the grocer's with a bottle of milk? Be careful how you answer and bear in mind the great effort I am making to regard you as human. . . .

BOBO: We know only too well what he'll become when he's drunk too much milk. And if we can't find a kid, then an old horse will do, or a dog or a doll.

VILLAGE: So it's always murder that we dream about?

ARCHIBALD: Always, and get going!

VILLAGE: (*to* VIRTUE, *though still hesitantly*). Come. Follow me. (*He starts leaving the stage, as if going down to join the audience.*) . . .

ARCHIBALD: (*holding them back*). No, no, that's not

33

necessary. Since we're on the stage, where everything is relative, all I need do is walk backwards in order to create the theatrical illusion of your moving away from me. Off I go. And I'm giving you rope enough to hang yourself, Mr. Wise-guy, by leaving you alone with that woman. You're on your own. The rest of us, let's go.

(ARCHIBALD, BOBO, DIOUF, SNOW *and* FELICITY *turn away and, holding their faces in their hands, move off, when suddenly nine or ten white masks suddenly appear about the Court.*)

VILLAGE: (*to* VIRTUE). I love you.

VIRTUE: Let's not rush matters, Village.

VILLAGE: I love you.

VIRTUE: That's an easy thing to say. An easy sentiment to feign, especially if it's limited to desire. You speak of love, but do you think we're alone? (*She points to the Court.*)

VILLAGE: (*alarmed*). As many as that!

VIRTUE: You insisted on being alone.

VILLAGE: (*more and more panicky*). But without them! Archibald! (*He cries out.*) Archibald! Bobo! (*They all remain unmoved.*) Snow! (*He rushes over to them, but they do not move. He comes back to* VIRTUE.) Virtue? They won't go away, will they?

VIRTUE: Don't be afraid. You wanted to love me. You spoke of leaving everything for. . . .

VILLAGE: I don't know whether I'll have the strength to. Now that they're here. . . .

VIRTUE: (*she puts her hand on his mouth*). Be still. First, let's love each other, if you have the strength to.

34

(*But the members of the Court seems to be getting excited, except for* THE QUEEN, *who is dozing. They stamp their feet, fidget, clap hands.*)

THE GOVERNOR: Damn it, they're going to gum up the works! Don't let them continue. (*To* THE QUEEN.) Madame, madame, wake up!

THE JUDGE: The Queen is asleep. (*With a finger to his lips.*) She's hatching. Hatching what? Celtic remains and the stained-glass windows of Chartres.

THE GOVERNOR: Damn it, wake her up. . . . Give her a dousing, the way they do at the barracks. . . .

THE JUDGE: You're out of your mind! Who'll do the hatching? You?

THE GOVERNOR: (*sheepishly*). I never knew how.

THE VALET: Neither did I. Especially standing up. For of course no one has seen my chair.

THE MISSIONARY: (*annoyed*). Nor mine. And I have to remain on my feet, although I'm a bishop-at-large. Nevertheless, they've got to be prevented from continuing. Listen. . . .

(*Below,* VILLAGE *and* VIRTUE, *who have been talking voicelessly, now continue aloud.*)

VILLAGE: Our colour isn't a wine-stain that blotches a face, our face isn't a jackal that devours those it looks at. . . . (*Shouting.*) I'm handsome, you're beautiful, and we love each other! I'm strong! If anyone touched you. . . .

VIRTUE: (*thrilled*). It would make me happy.

(VILLAGE *is taken aback.*)

THE GOVERNOR: (*to the Court*). Do you hear them? We've got to stop them. Right away. The Queen ought to speak. Madame, jump out of bed! (*He imitates with his mouth the bugle-call of reveille.*)

35

(THE JUDGE, THE MISSIONARY *and* THE VALET *are bent over* THE QUEEN. *They stand up straight, looking woebegone.*)

THE MISSIONARY: There's no doubt about it, she's snoring.

THE GOVERNOR: What about that great voice of hers? I'm listening.

(*A brief silence.*)

VIRTUE: (*softly, as if in a state of somnambulism*). I am the lily-white Queen of the West. Only centuries of breeding could achieve such a miracle! Immaculate, pleasing to the eye and to the soul! . . .

(*The entire Court listens attentively.*)

. . . Whether in excellent health, pink and gleaming, or consumed with languor, I am white. If death strikes me, I die in the colour of victory. Oh noble pallor, colour my temples, my fingers my belly! Oh eye of mine, delicately-shaded iris, bluish iris, iris of the glaciers, violet, hazel, grey-green, every-green iris, English lawn, Norman lawn, through you, but what do we see. . . .

(THE QUEEN, *who has finally awakened but is in a dazed state, listens to the poem and then recites along with* VIRTUE.)

. . . I am white, it's milk that symbolizes me, the lily, the dove, quicklime and the clear conscience, Poland with its eagle and snow! Snow. . . .

VILLAGE: (*suddenly lyrical*). Snow? If you like. Haunt me, lance-bearer. With my long dark strides I roamed the earth. Against that moving mass of darkness the angry but respectful sun flashed

36

its beams. They did not traverse my dusky
bulk. I was naked.

VIRTUE & THE QUEEN: (*together*). It's innocence and morning.

VILLAGE: The surfaces of my body were curved mirrors
in which all things were reflected: fish,
buffaloes, the laughter of tigers, reeds. Naked?
Or was my shoulder covered with a leaf? And
my member adorned with moss. . . .

VIRTUE & THE QUEEN: (*together*). . . . except that a bit of shade
remained in my armpits. . . .

VILLAGE: (*with rising frenzy*). . . . with moss, or seaweed?
I was not singing, I was not dancing. Standing
insolently—in short, royally—with hand on
hip, I was pissing. Oh! Oh! Oh! I crawled
through the cotton-plants. The dogs sniffed me
out. I bit my chains and wrists. Slavery taught
me dancing and singing.

VIRTUE: (*alone*). . . . a swarthy violet—almost black—
ring is spreading to my cheek. The night. . . .

VILLAGE: . . . I died in the hold of the slave ship. . . .

(VIRTUE *approaches him.*)

VIRTUE & THE QUEEN: I love you.

VILLAGE: I'm a long time dying.

THE QUEEN: (*suddenly wide awake*). That'll do! Silence them,
they've stolen my voice! Help! . . .

(*Suddenly* FELICITY *stands up. Everyone looks at
her and listens in silence.*)

FELICITY: Dahomey! . . . Dahomey! . . . Negroes from all
corners of the earth, to the rescue! Come!
Enter into me and only me! Swell me with your
tumult! Come barging in! Penetrate where you
will: my mouth, my ears—or my nostrils.

37

Nostrils, enormous conches, glory of my race, sunless shafts, tunnels, yawning grottoes where sniffling battalions lie at rest! Giantess with head thrown back, I await you all. Enter into me, ye multitudes, and be, for this evening only, my force and reason.

(*She sits down again. The dialogue continues.*)

THE QUEEN: (*very solemnly and almost swooning*). The hind that would be mated with the lion must die for love. . . .

THE VALET: Madame is dying!

THE QUEEN: Not yet! To the rescue, angel of the flaming sword, virgins of the Parthenon, stained-glass of Chartres, Lord Byron, Chopin, French cooking, the Unknown Soldier, Tyrolean songs, Aristotelian principles, heroic couplets, poppies, sunflowers, a touch of coquetry, vicarage gardens. . . .

THE ENTIRE COURT: Madame, we're here.

THE QUEEN: Ah, that's a comfort. I thought I'd been abandoned! They would have harmed me!

THE JUDGE: There's nothing to worry about. Our laws still hold.

THE MISSIONARY: (*to* THE QUEEN, *and facing her*). Have patience. We've only just begun the long death-struggle, which gives them such pleasure. Let's put a good face on it. It's in order to please them that we're going to die. . . .

THE QUEEN: Can't they hurry and get it over with? I'm weary and their odour is choking me. (*She pretends to be fainting.*)

THE MISSIONARY: Impossible. They've planned it down to the last detail, not in accordance with their own

38

THE QUEEN: (*in a dying voice*). And we're still too lively, aren't we? Yet all my blood's ebbing away.

(*At that moment,* ARCHIBALD, DIOUF, SNOW *and* BOBO *draw themselves up, turn about and move towards* VILLAGE.)

ARCHIBALD: Village, for the last time, I beseech you. . . .

VILLAGE: For the last time? This evening? (*With sudden decision.*) All right. This evening, for the last time. But you'll have to help me. Will you? Will you help me work myself up? Will you work me up?

SNOW: Me first, because I'm sick and tired of your cowardice.

VILLAGE: (*pointing to the catafalque*). It was I who killed her, and yet you accuse me.

SNOW: You had to bring yourself to do it.

VILLAGE: How do you know? You were hidden in the garden, you were waiting for me under the locust-tree. How could you have possibly seen me hesitating? While you were munching flowers in the twilight, I was bleeding her, without turning a hair.

SNOW: Yes, but you've been speaking about her lovingly ever since.

VILLAGE: Not about her, but about my gesture.

SNOW: You're lying!

VILLAGE: You're in love with me!

(*From this point on, the entire troupe becomes increasingly frenzied.*)

SNOW: You're lying. When you speak of her, such a

gentle expression, a look of such poignant
sadness comes over your thick lips and sick
eyes that I can see Nostalgia in person peeping
out. It wasn't your gesture that you were
describing when you spoke to me about her
lifted blue dress, nor your anger when you
described her mouth and teeth, nor the
resistance of the flesh to the knife when you
mentioned her weary eyelids, nor your nausea
when you told of how her body fell to the
rug. . . .

VILLAGE: You liar!

SNOW: . . . nor our sorrow when you thought of her
pallor, nor your fear of the police when you
outlined her ankles. You were talking of a great
love. From far off, from Ubangi or Tanganyika,
a tremendous love came here to die, to lick
white ankles. Negro, you were in love. Like a
sergeant in the marines. (*She drops to the floor,
exhausted, but* BOBO *and* ARCHIBALD *lift her up.*
BOBO *gives her a slap.*)

BOBO: (*holding up* SNOW'S *head, as if she were
vomiting*). Continue. Spill it all out. Spill it out!
Spill it out!

(VILLAGE *gets more and more irritated.*)

SNOW: (*as if trying to find more insults and vomiting
them forth, with hiccoughs*). Swear! Just as
others change their family or city or country or
name, just as they change gods, swear that it
never occurred to you to change colour in
order to attain her. But since you couldn't even
dream of royal white, you wished for a green
skin. . . . You've still got it!

VILLAGE: (*as if on edge*). You misunderstand completely.
In order to arouse her, to attract her, I had to

40

dance my nuptial flight. I beat my wing-sheaths. When it was over, I died, completely exhausted. My body was abandoned, and perhaps she entered while I was resting from my dance—or while I was dancing, who knows?

SNOW: So you admit!

VILLAGE: Not at all! All I know is that I killed her, since there she is (*pointing to the catafalque*). All I know is that one evening, when I went out hunting in the street, hunting the White-woman, I killed the one I brought back to you.

(*But they all turn their heads away.* MRS. FELICITY *steps down from her throne very majestically. She goes to the catafalque, bends down and slips a few grains under the sheet.*)

BOBO: Already!

FELICITY: I'm not stuffing her, you know. All the same, it's better for her not to dwindle away.

DIOUF: What do you feed her? Rice?

FELICITY: Corn. (*She silently returns to her place.*)

BOBO: Well, well, it's a long time since anyone's noticed Mr. Diouf. Look at how he's perked up. My word, he seems quite pleased with himself.

DIOUF: (*alarmed*). Madame. . . .

BOBO: What, Madame? Madame yourself. His eyes are gleaming. Does he already see his voluptuous bosom that the Negro lusts after.

DIOUF: (*frightened*). Madame! Bobo! It was wrong of me to have come this evening. Please let me go. Village is the one you ought to be concerned with. He's the one who has to be spurred on!

ARCHIBALD: We'll attend to Village. His crime saves him. If he committed it with hatred. . . ,

41

VILLAGE: (*screaming*). But it was with hatred! How can you doubt it? Are you all out of your mind? Tell me, ladies and gentlemen, are you crazy? She was standing behind her counter.

(*A long silence. The actors seem to be hanging from his lips.*)

SNOW: You said before: sitting at her sewing-machine.

VILLAGE: (*obstinately*). She was standing behind her counter.

BOBO: Well, what did she do?

(*They are all attentive.*)

VILLAGE: Negroes, I beseech you! She was standing. . . .

ARCHIBALD: (*gravely*). I order you to be black to your very veins. Pump black blood through them. Let Africa circulate in them. Let Negroes negrify themselves. Let them persist to the point of madness in what they're condemned to be, in their ebony, in their smell, in their yellow eyes, in their cannibal tastes. Let them not be content with eating Whites, but let them cook each other as well. Let them invent recipes for shin-bones, knee-caps, calves, thick lips, every-thing. Let them invent unknown sauces. Let them invent hiccoughs, belches and farts that'll give out a deleterious jazz. Let them invent a criminal painting and dancing. Negroes, if they change toward us, let it not be out of indulgence, but terror. (*To* DIOUF.) And you, Mr. Vicar General, for whom Christ died on the cross, you've got to make up your mind. (*To* VILLAGE.) As for Village, let him continue his spiel. So she was standing behind her counter. And what did she do? What did she say? And you, what did you do for us?

42

VILLAGE: (*pointing to* ARCHIBALD). She was standing there, where you are.

ARCHIBALD: (*stepping back*). No, no, not me.

VILLAGE: (*dancing in front of the coffin*). Then who? (*No one answers.*) Well, who? Now that she's dead, do you want me to open the coffin and repeat what I did with her when she was alive? You realize I'm supposed to re-enact it. I need a straight-man. This evening, I'm going through the whole thing. This evening, I'm giving a farewell performance. Who'll help me? Who? After all, it doesn't much matter who. As everyone knows, the Whites can hardly distinguish one Negro from another.

(*They all look at* FELICITY. *She hesitates, then draws herself up and speaks.*)

FELICITY: Mr. . . . Samba Graham Diouf! You're it.

DIOUF: (*frightened*). But Madame. . . .

FELICITY: This evening, you're the dead woman. Take your places.

(*Slowly and solemnly, each takes his place.* DIOUF *stands in front of the catafalque, facing the audience.*)

FELICITY: (*sitting down again*). Bring in the implements.

(BOBO *brings from behind the right screen a console-table on which are lying a blonde wig, a crude cardboard carnival mask representing a laughing white woman with big cheeks, a piece of pink knitting, two balls of wool, a knitting needle and white gloves.*)[1]

[1] In Blin's production—and Blin was right—these props were hooked on a vertical board and were visible to the audience from the very beginning. (Author's note)

FELICITY: Mr. Diouf, make your declaration. You know the formula, I take it.

DIOUF: (*facing the audience*). I, Samba Graham Diouf, born in the swamps of Ubangi Chari, sadly bid you farewell. I am not afraid. Open the door and I shall enter. I shall descend to the death you are preparing for me.

FELICITY: Good. Let's get on with the farewell.

(DIOUF *remains standing in front of the catafalque while the other actors line up toward the left and walk slowly backwards, gently waving small handkerchiefs which the men have drawn from their pockets and the women from their bosoms. Standing in line, they walk backwards very slowly about the catafalque, while* DIOUF, *facing the audience, keeps bowing to them in acknowledgement. In an undertone, they sing a kind of lullaby.*)

ALL: (*singing*).   Whistle gentle blackbirds
Nimble piccaninnies
Swimming in the water
Like any other birdies,
Birdies of the islands.
Charming little rascals
Be careful of the sharks
There's redness in the sky
Come back again and sleep
In shadows on the lawn
My tears and sobs will comfort me.

(DIOUF *bows and thanks them.*)

DIOUF: Your song was very beautiful, and your sadness does me honour. I'm going to start life in a new world. If ever I return, I'll tell you what it's like there. Great black country, I bid thee farewell. (*He bows.*)

44

ARCHIBALD: And now, ready for the mask!

DIOUF: (*grumblingly*). Are you sure we couldn't do without it? Look around you—people manage to do without all kinds of things, salt, tobacco, the Underground, women, even salted peanuts for cocktails and eggs for omelettes.

ARCHIBALD: I said let's get on with it. The implements.

(*The actors ceremoniously bring the wig, mask and gloves, with which they bedeck* DIOUF. *Thus adorned, he takes the knitting. While this goes on,* VILLAGE *gets impatient.*)

ARCHIBALD: (*to* VILLAGE). Carry on.

VILLAGE: (*stepping back, as if to judge the effect*). I'd gone to have a drink after work. . . .

BOBO: Stop! You're too pale. (*She runs to the shoeshine box and comes back to blacken* VILLAGE'S *face and hands, which she spits on and rubs.*)

BOBO: And if her teeth don't chatter now!

VILLAGE: So there she was . . . (*suddenly he stops and seems to be groping for words*). Are you sure there's any point in going straight through to the end?

SNOW: A little while ago you had no qualms about insulting me, and now you haven't strength enough to kill a white woman who's already dead.

BOBO: Snow's right. She's always right. Your hesitations throw us off. We were beginning to drool with impatience.

ARCHIBALD: (*angrily*). Take back that word, Bobo. No hysteria. This isn't a revival meeting, it's a ceremony.

45

BOBO: (*to the audience*). I beg your pardon, ladies. I beg your pardon, gentlemen.

VILLAGE: So there she was. . . . But, Negroes, you've forgotten the insults.

(*They all look at each other.*)

ARCHIBALD: So we have. He's right. You take it, Virtue. And roll them out, high and clear.

(*Bowing to* DIOUF, VIRTUE *recites a litany the way litanies of the Blessed Virgin are recited in church, in a monotone.*)

VIRTUE: LITANY OF THE LIVID
Livid as a t.b. death-rattle,
Livid as the droppings of a man with jaundice,
Livid as the belly of a cobra,
Livid as their convicts,
Livid as the god they nibble in the morning,
Livid as a knife in the night,
Livid . . . except: the English, Germans and
  Belgians, who are red . . . livid as jealousy.
Hail, the livid!

(VIRTUE *steps aside.* SNOW *takes her place and, after bowing to* DIOUF:)

SNOW: I, too, greet you, Tower of Ivory, Gate of Heaven flung wide open so that the Negro can enter, majestic and smelly. But how livid you are! What malady consumes you? Will you play Camille this evening? Wondrous, indeed, the malady that makes you ever whiter and that leads you to ultimate whiteness. (*She bursts out laughing.*) But what's that I see flowing down your black stockings? So it was true, Lord Jesus, that behind the mask of a cornered White is a poor trembling negro. (*She steps back and says to* BOBO.) Take it.

46

BOBO: Let's both take it! (*She tucks up her skirt and does an obscene dance.*)

ARCHIBALD: All right. Take it, Village.

VILLAGE: I don't know whether I'll be able. . . .

ARCHIBALD: (*furiously*). What? Changing tone again? Whom are you talking to? What are you talking about? This is the theatre, not the street. The theatre, and drama, and crime.

VILLAGE: (*with sudden fury, he seems about to spring forward, makes a gesture as if to thrust everyone aside*). Stand aside! Here I come! (*He had stepped back, and now moves forward.*) I enter. And I fart. Lumbering along on my thighs, cast-iron columns. And I breeze in. I take a look around. . . .

BOBO: You're lying. Last night you entered slyly, very cautiously. You're distorting things.

VILLAGE: (*continuing*). I enter, and I approach, softly. I take a furtive peep. I look about me. To the right. To the left. "How do you do, Madame?" (*He bows to* DIOUF, *who, with the knitting in his hand, returns the bow.*) How do you do, Madame? It's not warm. (*They all cock their ears to hear what the Mask says. He stops talking, but the actors must have heard him, for they raise their heads and laugh, with their orchestrated laugh.*) It's not warm. I've made so bold as to come in for a moment. Here at least it's nice and comfortable. Are you knitting a helmet? A pink one? The light is very soft. It suits your pretty face. Yes, I'll have a glass of rum. I'll have a nip. (*In a different tone, addressing the* NEGROES.) That the right tone?

ALL: (*breathlessly*). Yes!

47

VILLAGE: The moon—for it was almost night—rose artfully over a landscape inhabited by insects. It's a distant land, madame, but my whole body could sing it. Listen to the singing! Listen! (*Suddenly he breaks off and points to the Mask, who is knitting.*) But he's not wearing a skirt! What kind of masquerade is that? I'll stop my speech if you don't put a skirt on him.

ARCHIBALD: Snow, your shawl. . . .

SNOW: My net shawl? He'll step on it and tear it.

ARCHIBALD: Well, hasn't anyone got something to give him?

(*They are all silent. Suddenly FELICITY stands up. She takes off her skirt and tosses it to DIOUF.*)

FELICITY: Slip it on. It'll hide your shoes.

(DIOUF *stops knitting. He is helped on with the skirt.*)

VILLAGE: I'll go back a little. . . . "The moon. . . ."

BOBO: No, you've already recited that.

VILLAGE: (*resignedly*). All right. I continue. Listen to the singing of my thighs. . . . Because . . . (*a rather long pause, during which he pretends to have an important revelation to make*) . . . because my thighs fascinated her. (*Fatuously.*) Ask her. (*The NEGROES go to the Mask and whisper in his ear. The Mask remains silent, but the NEGROES burst out laughing.*) You see! She even has the nerve to boast of it! (*A pause.*) But that's not all, it has to raise a laugh! From the attic, where her bed was, I could hear her mother calling for her evening medicine. (*A brief pause; then, to FELICITY.*) Well, that's your cue. Play the Mother.

FELICITY: (*imitating a plaintive patient, with her eyes to the*

48

ceiling). Ma-a-rie! Maa-a-arie! Daughter, it's
time for my sugared almonds and aspirin! And
it's prayer-time.

(*The Mask seems to be moving toward the voice.
He takes a few short steps in the direction of*
FELICITY, *but* VILLAGE *calmly and sternly steps
between them.*)

VILLAGE: (*assuming a woman's voice*). Yes, mother dear,
right away. The water's heating. I'll iron another
couple of sheets and then bring up your
sugared almonds. (*To the Mask.*) Take it easy,
girlie. You don't give a damn about the old
hag. Any more than I do. She's had her day. To
hell with her and her sugared almonds. If
you're heating water, it's for after the fun.
What's the matter, what's. . . .

FELICITY: Ma-a-arie! My darling little daughter. It's time
for my sugared almonds. When your father was
still a magistrate, he always used to bring me
one at this time of day, in the gloaming. Don't
leave me alone in the attic. (*A pause.*) And don't
forget, the baker's wife's coming.

ARCHIBALD: (*to* BOBO, *whom he pushes toward the right wing*).
Your cue. Enter.

(BOBO, *who has stepped back to the wing, enters
hesitantly, as if she were in a procession.*)

BOBO: (*acting the neighbour*). Good evening, Marie.
Aren't you in? Goodness me, how dark it is. As
our constable would say, in that roguish way of
his, it's as dark here as up a nigger's hole. Oh! I
beg your pardon—I mean a negro's. One should
be polite. (*A pause.*) What, you're checking the
day's accounts? All right, then I'll come back
tomorrow. I know what that's like. I'm a

sensible person. Goodbye, Marie, and good
night.

(*She mimes all the gestures of departure, but
remains on-stage, near the wing, looking off-stage
and fixed in an attitude of departure.*)

VILLAGE: (*resuming the formal tone of his recital*). So there
I was, nestling in the shadow. And I whispered
to her: Listen to the singing of my thighs!
Listen! (*He makes his thighs bulge under his
trousers.*) That sound is the mewing of panthers
and tigers. When they bend, that means
leopards are stretching. If I unbutton, an eagle
of the Great Empire will swoop down from our
snowy summits to your Pyrenees. But . . . I'm
not dead-set on unbuttoning. The fires are
being lit. Under our dry fingers, the drums. . . .

(*They all start dancing in place—even* BOBO, *who
is looking into the wings, even the Court, but not
the Mask—and clapping their hands very softly.*)

Then, in the glade, the dance began! (*Turning to
the others.*) For I had to cast a spell on her,
didn't I? My aim, then, was to draw her gently
toward her room. The door of the shop opened
out into the street, the old bitch was dying
upstairs. . . .

FELICITY: (*imitating the old mother*). Almonds!
A-a-almonds! Prayers! Pra-a-ayers! It's time
for your prayer! Don't forget!

VILLAGE: (*very annoyed*). She's going to spoil everything.
(*Re-assuming the woman's voice.*) I have one
more layette to finish, mother dear, and then
I'll be right up. (*Resuming the formal tone of his
recital.*) I asked for another glass of rum. The
liquor kindled my genius. I was feeling, as they
say, a little high. In my eye I trotted out a big

50

parade of our warriors, diseases, alligators,
amazons, straw-huts, cataracts, hunts, cotton,
even leprosy and even a hundred thousand
youngsters who died in the dust. Along my
teeth I set adrift our pointiest canoes. With a
hand in my pocket, as if I were going to dance
the tango, I went up to her and said, "Kind
lady, it's nasty outside." She replied:

(*As before, they all listen to the Mask, who says
nothing. Then they burst out in their orchestrated
laugh.*)

. . . Yes, you're quite right. We must be careful.
People gossip in small towns. . . .

BOBO: (*pretending to return and to want to enter the
shop*). Marie, you still haven't put the light on.
You'll spoil your eyes working in the dark. (*A
pause.*) I hear someone whistling on the road.
It's probably your husband. Good night,
Marie.

(*Same pantomime as before. All this time,
VILLAGE has been looking as if he were very much
afraid of being discovered.*)

VILLAGE: (*tone of the recital.*) Indeed, one can never be
too careful: suns revolve about the earth. . . .

FELICITY: (*imitating the old mother*). Ma-a-arie!
A-a-almonds! Beware of the night, child. All
cats are black in the dark, and one forgets to
give the evening almond to one's old mother. (*A
pause.*) Tell your sister Susan to come in.

VILLAGE: (*assuming the voice of a woman*). Susan! Susan!
Where are you?

SNOW: (*who has run behind the catafalque, where she is
hidden*). Why, I'm here. I'm in the garden.

VILLAGE: (*holding back the Mask, who seems to want to go toward the catafalque, and still imitating a woman's voice*). Are you all alone in the garden?

THE MISSIONARY: (*to* ARCHIBALD). Your cue, Archibald.

(ARCHIBALD *runs to the left wing, from which he now seems to be entering very casually, whistling as he walks. However, he merely imitates the movement of walking and actually remains where he is.*)

SNOW: I'm all alone, all by myself. I'm playing knuckle-bones.

VILLAGE: (*still in a woman's voice*). Be careful, Susan, watch out for prowlers. It hasn't been safe in these parts ever since they began recruiting aviators in Guiana.

VOICE OF SNOW: In Guiana! Aviators!

VILLAGE: (*voice of the recital*). In Guiana, you slut! . . . suns revolve about the earth, eagles swoop down on our battlefields . . . so let's close the window. She acted as if she didn't understand. Gallantly I closed the window. Snow was falling on the town.

VIRTUE: (*rushing toward him in a panic*). Stop it!

BOBO: (*still fixed in a movement of departure, but turning her head to blurt out the following*). Look how he's carrying on. He's foaming. He's fuming. It's a mirage!

VIRTUE: Village, Village, please, I'm asking you, stop.

VILLAGE: (*looking at* VIRTUE). The limpidity of your blue eyes, that tear gleaming at the corner, your heavenly bosom. . . .

VIRTUE: You're raving. Whom are you talking to?

52

VILLAGE: (*still looking at* VIRTUE). I love you and I can't
bear it any longer.

VIRTUE: (*screaming*). Village!

SNOW: (*peeping out from behind the catafalque just long
enough to say the following*). But, my dear, it has
nothing to do with you, you might have
realized it.

VILLAGE: (*turning slowly to the Mask, who mechanically
goes on with his knitting*). Your feet, the soles of
which are the colour of periwinkles, your feet,
which are varnished on top, walked along the
pavement . . ..

VIRTUE: You've already said that to me. Stop talking.

ARCHIBALD: (*breaking off his silent whistling and immobile
walk and assuming an angry expression*).
Negroes, I'm losing my temper. Either we
continue the re-enactment or we leave.

VILLAGE: (*imperturbably, now fully facing the Mask*). The
gentlest of your movements delineate you so
exquisitely that when I'm on your shoulder I
feel you're being borne by the wind. The rings
under your eyes distress me. Madame, when
you go . . . go on. (*To the audience.*) For she
wasn't coming, she was going. She was going to
her bedroom. . . .

FELICITY: (*imitating the old woman*). My almond and my
prayer!

VOICE OF SNOW: Yes, yes, I'm alone in the garden, astride the
jet of water.

BOBO: (*seeming to come back*). Good evening, Marie.
Lock your door.

VILLAGE: (*voice of the recital*). . . . to her bedroom,
where I followed her in order to strangle her.

53

(*To the Mask.*) Get going, slut. And go wash yourself. (*To the audience.*) I had to work fast, the cuckold was on his way.

(*The Mask is about to start walking.*)

Stop! (*To the audience.*) But first let me show you what I was able to get out of my tamed captive. . . .

THE JUDGE: But what's Virtue's role in the crime?

(ARCHIBALD *and* BOBO *turn their heads.* SNOW *shows hers. They seem very much interested.*)

VILLAGE: (*after a moment's hesitation*). None. She never ceased to be present, at my side, in her immortal form. (*To the audience.*) . . . my tamed captive. For she was clever and highly reputed among those of her race. Come. Stand in a circle. (*He pretends to be speaking both to the audience and to invisible Negroes on the stage.*) Not too close. There. Now I'm going to make her work. (*To the Mask.*) Are you ready, kid?

THE JUDGE: No, no. It's better to maintain a formal tone.

VILLAGE: Do you really want me to?

THE JUDGE: Yes, it's better. Don't be afraid to establish distance.

VILLAGE: As you like. (*To the audience.*) She can play the piano. Very, very well. Would anyone like to hold her knitting for a moment?

(*He addresses the audience directly, until a spectator comes up and takes the needle from the Mask's hands.*)

(*To the spectator.*) Thank you, sir (*or* "madame"). (*To the Mask.*) Now play us a Strauss melody.

54

(*The Mask docilely sits down on an invisible
stool and, facing the audience, plays on an
invisible piano.*)

Stop! (*He stops playing. The Court applauds.*)

THE QUEEN: (*simperingly*). Perfect, perfect, she was almost
too perfect. Even in adversity, in disaster, our
melodies will sing.

THE VALET: (*to* VILLAGE). What else can she do?

VILLAGE: As you've seen, she knits helmets for little
chimney-sweeps. On Sunday she sings at the
harmonium. She prays. (*To the Mask.*) On your
knees! (*He kneels.*) With your hands clasped.
Eyes upward. Good. Pray! (*The entire Court
applauds in elegant fashion.*) She's good at lots
of other things. She does water-colours and
rinses glasses.

FELICITY: (*voice of the old mother*). Marie! Ma-a-arie! My
a-a-almond! Child, it's time for it.

VILLAGE: (*woman's voice*). Right away, mother dear. I've
almost finished rinsing the glasses. (*Voice of the
recital.*) One day she even roasted in the
flames. . . .

THE COURT: (*except* THE MISSIONARY). Speed it up, talk faster!

THE MISSIONARY: How dare you allude to that wicked affair.

THE VALET: (*to* THE MISSIONARY). Haven't you placed her in
heaven since then?

THE QUEEN: But, what do they mean?

VILLAGE: One day they caught her as she was wheeling
about on her horse amidst the banners. They
put her into prison and burned her at the stake.

SNOW: (*showing her head, and, with a burst of laughter*).
Then they ate the pieces.

THE QUEEN: (*with a piercing cry*). My saint! (*Exit, hiding her face and sobbing her heart out;* THE VALET *accompanies her.*)

VILLAGE: But, for the most part, she does what she can. When the time comes, she calls the midwife. . . . (*To* BOBO.) Take it, Bobo.

(BOBO *approaches the Mask and speaks to him gently*).

BOBO: You'd better lie down so that it doesn't hurt too much. (*She listens to the Mask, who makes no answer.*) Your pride? . . . All right. Remain standing.

(*She kneels and puts her hand under the Mask's skirt, from where she takes out a doll about two feet long representing the Governor.*)

THE GOVERNOR: (*to the Court*). I'm entering the world! With boots on, decorated. . . .

(BOBO *keeps searching and pulls out another doll:* THE VALET.)

THE VALET: Here comes my mug!

(BOBO *searches and takes out* THE JUDGE.)

THE JUDGE: (*in amazement*). Me?

THE GOVERNOR: (*to* THE JUDGE). It's the spitting image of you!

(BOBO *pulls out* THE MISSIONARY.)

THE MISSIONARY: The ways of Providence. . . .

(BOBO *takes out a doll representing* THE QUEEN.)

THE QUEEN: (*re-entering just as the doll emerges*). I'd like to see myself come out of there. . . . There I come! My mother spawned me standing up! (*Exit.*)

(*The* NEGROES *have hung up the dolls on the left*

56

side of the stage, under the Court's balcony.
They gaze at them and then resume their recital.)

SNOW: (*still fixed in an attitude of departure, as if about to enter the right wing; turning her head*). In any event, the one who's rotting in the packing-case never had such a high old time.

(*Exit* THE GOVERNOR.)

VILLAGE: Let's forget about her. (*To the spectator who is holding the knitting.*) Give her back her knitting. Thank you, sir. You may go. (*The spectator returns to his seat.*) (*To the Mask.*) And now, let's continue. Go on, madame. . . .

(*The Mask starts walking very slowly toward the right screen.*)

Walk! This evening you have the noblest gait in the realm. (*To the audience.*) As you see, the husband arrived too late. He'll find only his wife's corpse, disembowelled but still warm. (*To the Mask, who had stopped but who starts walking again.*) It's no longer a negro trailing at your skirt; it's a marketful of slaves, all sticking out their tongues. Just because you've kindly given me a drink of rum you think . . . eh, you bitch! Pull me toward your lace. . . . (*They both move toward the screen, very slowly, the Mask in front of* VILLAGE.) . . . Underneath you're surely wearing some sort of black petticoat that's silkier than my gaze. . . .

VIRTUE: (*falling to her knees*). Village!

VILLAGE: (*to the Mask*). Walk faster, I'm in a hurry. Follow the corridor. Turn right. Good. You know the door of your room. Open it. How gracefully you walk, oh noble and familiar rump!

57

(They mount the steps and are about to go behind the screen. But before following the Mask there, VILLAGE *turns to the audience.)*

Are they following me? *(To the* NEGROES.) Are you following me?

(The NEGROES, *that is,* ARCHIBALD, BOBO *and* SNOW—VIRTUE *remains kneeling—place themselves behind him, in a procession, softly clapping their hands and stamping their feet.)*

But if I go too far, stop me.

(Enter THE GOVERNOR.)

THE JUDGE: What's the Queen doing?

THE GOVERNOR: She's weeping, sir. Torrents are pouring from her eyes and flowing down to the plains, which, alas, they cannot fertilize, for the water is warm and salty.

THE MISSIONARY: Does she have need of religion?

THE VALET: I'll go and console her. I know how to handle her.

ALL: *(except* VIRTUE, *to* VILLAGE). We'll help you. Don't be afraid. Keep walking.

VILLAGE: *(imploringly).* Tell me, Negroes, what if I couldn't stop?

ALL: *(except* VIRTUE). Keep going.

BOBO: The Valet has set an example for you. He's already with the Queen.

VILLAGE: *(falling on one knee).* Negroes, I beg of you. . . .

BOBO: *(laughing).* Inside with you, you lazy lubber!

SNOW: *(kneeling).* Pour forth torrents. First, showers of sperm and then streams of her blood. *(Cupping her hands*.) I'll drink it, Village, I'll wash my chin with it, my belly, my shoulders.

VILLAGE: (*a white-gloved hand, that of the Mask, who is behind the screen, comes down on his shoulder and remains there*). Friends, friends, I beg of you. . . .

ALL: (*still clapping their hands and stamping their feet gently*). Go on in. She's already lying down. She's put aside her knitting. She's calling for your big ebony body. She has blown out the candle. She's darkening the room to put you at ease!

VILLAGE: Friends. . . .

FELICITY: (*suddenly standing up straight*). Dahomey! Dahomey! To my rescue, Negroes, all of you! Gentlemen of Timbuctoo, come in, under your white parasols! Stand over there. Tribes covered with gold and mud, rise up from my body, emerge! Tribes of the Rain and Wind, forward! Princes of the Upper Empires, of the bare feet and wooden stirrups, on your caparisoned horses, enter! Enter on horseback. Gallop in! Gallop in! Hop it! Hop it! Hop along! Negroes of the ponds, you who fish with your pointed beaks, enter! Negroes of the docks, of the factories, of the dives, Negroes of the Ford plant, Negroes of General Motors, and you, too, negroes who braid rushes to encage crickets and roses, enter and remain standing! Conquered soldiers, enter. Conquering soldiers, enter. Crowd in. More. Lay your shields against the walls. You, too, who dig up corpses to suck the brains from skulls, enter unashamedly. You, tangled brother-sister, walking melancholy incest, come in. Barbarians, barbarians, barbarians, come along. I can't describe you

59

all, nor even name you all, nor name your
dead, your arms, your ploughs, but enter.
Walk gently on your white feet. White? No,
black. Black or white? Or blue? Red, green,
blue, white, red, green, yellow, who knows,
where am I? The colours exhaust me. . . . Are
you there, Africa with the bulging chest and
oblong thigh? Sulking Africa, wrought of iron,
in the fire, Africa of the millions of royal slaves,
deported Africa, drifting continent, are you
there? Slowly you vanish, you withdraw into
the past, into the tales of castaways, colonial
museums, the works of scholars, but I call you
back this evening to attend a secret revel.
(*Pondering.*) It's a block of darkness, compact
and evil, that holds its breath, but not its odour.
Are you there? Don't leave the stage unless I
tell you to. Let the spectators behold you. A
deep, almost invisible somnolence emanates
from you, spreads all about, hypnotizes them.
We shall presently go down amongst them, but
before we do. . . .

VILLAGE: Madame. . . .

FELICITY: . . . but before we do, allow me to introduce the
most cowardly of all negroes. Need I name
him? (*To* VILLAGE.) Well, get going.

VILLAGE: (*trembling. The white-gloved hand is still resting
on his shoulder*). Madame. . . .

FELICITY: If he's still hesitating, let him take the place of
the dead woman. (*She sits down, exhausted.*)

VILLAGE & VIRTUE: (*together*). No!

ARCHIBALD: (*to* VILLAGE). Go on in.

VILLAGE: (*to the melody of the "Dies Irae"*). Madame . . .
Madame. . . .

SNOW: (*to the "Dies Irae"*). Enter, enter . . . deliver us
from evil. Hallelujah. . . .

BOBO: (*all the speeches will now be sung to the same
melody*). Oh descend, my cataracts!

VILLAGE: Madame . . . Madame. . . .

SNOW: I still snow upon your countryside,
I still snow upon your tombs, and I calm you. . . .

VIRTUE: The north winds have been forewarned:
Let them load it on their shoulders
All the horses are untethered.

VILLAGE: (*still kneeling; moving backwards, as if drawn
by the white-gloved hand, he disappears behind
the screen, where the Mask is*). Madame . . .
Madame. . . .

VIRTUE: And thou, evening twilight,
Weave the cloak that shrouds him.

SNOW: Expire, expire gently,
Our Lady of the Pelicans,
Pretty seagull, politely,
Gallantly, let yourself be tortured. . . .

VIRTUE: Beshroud yourselves, tall forests,
That he may steal in silently,
Shoe his big feet, oh white dust, with felt
slippers.

THE JUDGE: (*to* THE GOVERNOR, *who is looking through his
spy-glass at what is going on behind the screen*).
What do you make out?

THE GOVERNOR: Nothing out of the ordinary. (*Laughing.*) The
woman is giving in. You can say what you like
about them, but those fellows are terrific
f—ers.

THE MISSIONARY: You're forgetting yourself, my dear governor.

61

THE GOVERNOR: I'm sorry. I mean that the flesh is weak. It's a law of nature.

THE JUDGE: But what is it they're doing? Describe it.

THE GOVERNOR: Now he's washing his hands . . . he's drying them . . . those people are clean. I've always noticed that. When I was a lieutenant, my orderly. . . .

THE JUDGE: What else is he doing?

THE GOVERNOR: He's smiling . . . he's taking out his pack of Chesterfields . . . puff! He's blown out the candle.

THE JUDGE: Not really?

THE GOVERNOR: Take the spy-glass, or the lantern, and have a look.

(THE JUDGE *shrugs his shoulders.*)

ARCHIBALD: (*suddenly aware of the presence of* NEWPORT NEWS, *who entered very slowly while* FELICITY *was delivering her long speech*). You! I told you to come back and let us know only when everything was finished. So it's over? It's done? (*Turning to the Court, all of whose members have put their hands to their faces, he screams.*) Keep your masks on!

NEWPORT NEWS: Not quite. He's defending himself as best he can, but he'll certainly be executed.

ARCHIBALD: (*he has changed his voice. Instead of declaiming, he speaks in his natural tone*). The shot'll make a noise. (*A pause.*) Are you sure he's guilty? And are you sure he's the one we've been looking for?

NEWPORT NEWS: (*a little ironically*). Are you suddenly getting suspicious?

62

ARCHIBALD: Bear in mind that it's a matter of judging and probably sentencing and executing a negro. That's a serious affair. It's no longer a matter of acting. The man we're holding and for whom we're responsible is a real man. He moves, he chews, he coughs, he trembles. In a little while, he'll be killed.

NEWPORT NEWS: That's very tough. But though we can put on an act in front of them (*pointing to the audience*), we've got to stop acting when we're among ourselves. We'll have to get used to taking responsibility for blood—our own. And the moral weight. . . .

ARCHIBALD: All the same, as I've said, it's a matter of living blood, hot, supple, reeking blood, of blood that bleeds. . . .

NEWPORT NEWS: But then what about the act we put on? Was it just an entertainment, as far as you were concerned? Its purpose wasn't to give a detailed. . . .

ARCHIBALD: (*interrupting him*). Be quiet. (*A pause.*) Is he going to be executed?

NEWPORT NEWS: He is.

ARCHIBALD: All right. Go back to them.

NEWPORT NEWS: I need to be here. In any case, it's too late. Let me go through with it. Here.

ARCHIBALD: Well . . . then stay. (*to the* NEGRESSES). And you, be quiet. Village is working for us. Help him in silence, but help him.

(*Enter* THE VALET.)

THE GOVERNOR: What about the Queen? What's she doing?

THE VALET: She's still crying. It's the warm rains of September.

THE GOVERNOR: And . . . what did she say?

THE VALET: At least save the child! And see to it that the mother is received courteously. She has gone astray, but she's a white woman.

(*A very long silence.*)

VIRTUE: (*timidly*). He hasn't come back.

BOBO: (*in an undertone*). He hasn't had time to. After all, it's far away.

VIRTUE: What do you mean far away? It's behind the screen.

BOBO: (*still in an undertone, slightly annoyed*). Of course. But at the same time they've got to go elsewhere. They have to cross the room, go through the garden, take a path lined with hazel trees, turn left, push aside the thorns, throw salt in front of them, put on boots, enter the woods. . . . It's night time. Deep in the woods. . . .

THE GOVERNOR: Gentlemen, we've got to start getting ready. Wake the Queen. We must go and punish them, we must try them, and the journey will be long and arduous.

THE MISSIONARY: I'll need a horse.

THE VALET: Everything has been attended to, monsignor.

BOBO: (*resuming*) . . . deep in the woods, look for the gate of the cavern, find the key, go down the steps . . . dig the grave. . . . Flee. Will the moon wait? All that takes time. You yourself, when you go upstairs with the gentleman who's on his way home from his wife's funeral. . . .

VIRTUE: (*curtly.*) You're right. I do a conscientious job. But Village ought to have acted it out before our eyes.

64

BOBO: Greek tragedy, my dear, decorum. The ultimate gesture is performed off-stage.

ARCHIBALD: (*irritated, makes a threatening gesture to them and points to* VILLAGE, *who enters*). Ladies, I told you to be quiet.

(*A rather long silence. Then, enter* VILLAGE, *quietly. His shirt-collar is awry. They all surround him.*)

ARCHIBALD: Is it over. Did you have much trouble?

VILLAGE: Same as usual.

SNOW: Nothing happened, did it?

VILLAGE: No, nothing. Or, if you prefer, it all went off as usual, and very smoothly. When Diouf entered behind the screen, he kindly offered me a seat.

SNOW: And then?

NEWPORT NEWS: Nothing else. They waited on a bench, off-stage, and smiled at each other in amusement.

VILLAGE: (*catching sight of* NEWPORT NEWS). Are you back? You should still be there, with them. . . .

NEWPORT NEWS: I thought that this evening, thanks to you, everything was supposed to change, and that this would be the last night.

VILLAGE: (*annoyed*). I did what I could. But what about you? What about them?

NEWPORT NEWS: What they do is no business of yours. It's for *them* to ask questions. But . . . I'm glad you performed the rite, as you do every evening. It'll be my job to finish off the performance.

ARCHIBALD: There's nothing new, at least, in the ceremony.

NEWPORT NEWS: (*angrily*). Do you want to continue it for ever

65

and ever? To perpetuate it until the death of the race? As long as the earth revolves about the sun, which is itself carried off in a straight line to the very limits of God, in a secret chamber, Negroes will. . . .

BOBO: (*screaming*). Will hate! Yessir!

THE JUDGE: (*to the Court*). I think we have no more time to waste.

(*A singing is heard—a kind of solemn march, which is sung. Then,* THE QUEEN *appears, leading* DIOUF, *who is masked and wearing his trappings.*)

THE QUEEN: This is the woman whom we must go down and avenge.

THE QUEEN: (*to* DIOUF). The journey must have been arduous, poor child. At last you're with your true family. From here, from on high, you'll have a better view of them.

THE MISSIONARY: When we get back, we'll try to beatify her.

THE VALET: A terrific idea! Her Majesty will adopt her. Won't she, child ?

THE QUEEN: We'll have to think about that. It's a very delicate matter. After all, she *has* been defiled. Against her will, I hope, but, after all, she's liable to be a reminder of our shame. (*After a hesitation.*) However, the idea is worth considering. (*To* THE JUDGE.) What are they doing down there?

THE JUDGE: (*looking with* THE GOVERNOR'S *field-glass*). They're wild with anger, with rage, and somewhat confused.

THE QUEEN: What are they saying?

THE JUDGE: They're utterly dumbfounded.

THE QUEEN: But . . . what's going on that's so strange and rare? Is snow falling on their mangroves?

THE JUDGE: Madame . . . it may be that a crime is being committed.

THE QUEEN: No doubt.

THE JUDGE: No, another one. One that's being judged elsewhere.

THE QUEEN: But—what can we do? Prevent it? Or make use of it?

(*The members of the Court all lean forward.*)

VILLAGE: (*to* ARCHIBALD). Are they going to come, sir? Are they coming to judge us, to weigh us? (VILLAGE *is trembling.*)

ARCHIBALD: (*putting his hand on* VILLAGE's *shoulder*). Don't be afraid. It's only play-acting.

VILLAGE: (*persisting*). To weigh us? With their golden and ruby scales? And do you think, if they go off to die, that they'll let me love Virtue—or rather that Virtue will be able to love me?

NEWPORT NEWS: (*smiling, but pointedly*). Didn't you try to negrify them? To graft Bambara lips and nostrils on them? To kink their hair? To reduce them to slavery?

THE MISSIONARY: (*roaring out*). Off we go! And not another minute to waste. (*To* THE VALET.) Prepare the cloak and boots, a pound of cherries and Her Majesty's horse. (*To* THE QUEEN.) Madame, we must be off. It will be a long journey. (*To* THE GOVERNOR.) Have you the umbrellas?

THE GOVERNOR: (*hurt*). Ask Joseph. (*To* THE VALET.) Have you the flask?

THE VALET: On getting out of bed, the Queen knighted me

67

and gave me a title. And don't forget it. All the same, I have the umbrellas and the quinine tablets. I also have a flask of rum—full to the brim! Because it'll be hot.

THE MISSIONARY: During the trek, I authorize drinking to beguile fatigue, and let a Palestrina Mass be sung. Everyone ready? Then, forward . . . march!

(*The entire Court disappears, leaving the platform, where* DIOUF, *still masked, remains alone. At first, he hesitates, then, timidly, approaches the hand-rail and looks down.*)
(*The Court remains off-stage for four or five minutes. The* NEGROES *below have gathered together, left. In front of the group stands* NEWPORT NEWS. *They are all waiting anxiously.* BOBO *raises her head. She sees* DIOUF *leaning over the rail and looking at them.*)

BOBO: You! You, Mr. Diouf?

(*The* NEGROES *all raise their heads and look at* DIOUF, *who, still masked, nods "yes".*)

Mr. Diouf, you're living a curious death. What's it like there?

DIOUF: (*slowly removing his mask*). The light there is rather queer.

BOBO: Tell us, Mr. Vicar General, what do you see there? Answer, Diouf. Seen through their eyes, what are their kings like? What do you see from the height of your blue eyes, from the height of those belvederes?

DIOUF: (*hesitating*). I see you—sorry—I see us as follows: I'm on high, and not on the ground. And I am perhaps experiencing the vision of God.

68

BOBO: Are you a white woman?

DIOUF: The first thing to tell you is that they lie or that they're mistaken. They're not white, but pink or yellowish.

BOBO: Then are you a pink woman?

DIOUF: I am. I move about in a light emitted by our faces which they reflect from one to another. We, that is, you, we're still suffocating in a heavy atmosphere. It all began when I had to leave your world. I was eaten with despair. But your insults and homage little by little exalted me. I was imbued with a new life. I felt Village's desire. His voice was so rough! And his gaze! Humble and triumphant. Before I knew it, I was with child by him.

BOBO: Are you proud?

DIOUF: Proud, no. Our cares and concerns no longer have meaning for me. New relationships come into being along with new things, and these things become necessary. (*Pensively*.) Indeed, necessity is a very curious novelty. The harmony thrills me. I had left the realm of gratuitousness where I saw you gesticulating. I could no longer see even our hatred, our hatred which rises up to them. I learned, for example, that they're able to perform true dramas and to believe in them.

NEWPORT NEWS: (*ironically*). You miss those days of the dead, don't you?

ARCHIBALD: Every actor knows that at a given time the curtain will fall. And that he almost always embodies a dead man or dead woman: Lady Macbeth, Don Giovanni, Antigone, Camille, Dr. Schweitzer. . . .

69

(*A long silence.*)

(*Footsteps are heard off-stage.* DIOUF, *in a panic, puts on his mask again. The other* NEGROES *seem frightened. All of them, in a body, including* MRS. FELICITY, *go to the left side of the stage and huddle under the balcony where the Court had been. The sound of footsteps becomes more distinct. At length, from the right wing, as if coming down a road, emerges first* THE VALET, *walking backwards. He is belching and staggering. He is obviously drunk.*)

THE VALET: (*facing the wing; belching*). Be careful with the nag! See that he doesn't stumble. The Queen's not going (*belches*) to arrive on a horse with broken knees. Oh, bishop-at-large, be careful that the train of the Queen's cloak and your (*belches*) white (*belches*) purple skirt don't get caught in the cactus. Damn it, what dust! Mouth's full of it! But you. . . . (*Belches*) Gives you a certain air! Watch out . . . watch out . . . there . . . there. . . . (*He makes a gesture as if to indicate the road to take.*)

(*Finally, also walking backwards, appear* THE GOVERNOR, THE MISSIONARY, THE JUDGE, *and then, moving forward,* THE QUEEN. *She seems very weary, as after a long journey. They are all drunk.*)

THE QUEEN: (*unsteady on her legs and advancing cautiously, looking about her*). Dust! Mouth's full of it, but it gives you a certain air! (*She belches and bursts out laughing.*) Look where it gets us, following old troopers under colonial skies. (*She takes the empty flask and throws it away.*) And not a drop left. (*Belches.*) (*Suddenly noble.*) Thus do I set my foot on my foreign possessions. (*Laughs.*)

70

THE GOVERNOR: (*hiccoughing after each word*). Stop in your
tracks. Prudence, circumspection, mystery. All
is swamp, quagmires, arrows, felines. . . .

(*Very softly at first, then more and more loudly,
the* NEGROES, *almost invisible under the balcony,
utter sounds of the virgin forest: croaking of the
toad, hoot of the owl, a hissing, very gentle roars,
breaking of wood, moaning of the wind.*)

. . . here, from the skin of their bellies the snakes
lay eggs from which blinded children take
wing . . . the ants riddle you with vinegar or
arrows . . . the creepers fall madly in love with
you, kiss your lips and eat you . . . here the
rocks float . . . the water is dry . . . the wind is a
skyscraper . . . all is leprosy, sorcery, danger,
madness. . . .

THE QUEEN: (*wonderstruck*). And flowers!

THE JUDGE: (*hiccoughing*). Poisonous, Madame. Deadly.
Sick. Drank too much rum. Leaden sky,
Madame. Our pioneers tried grafts on our
garden cabbage, on the Dutch peony, on
rhubarb. Our plants died, Madame, murdered
by those of the tropics.

(*The* NEGROES *laugh with their orchestrated
laugh, very softly. They start making their
sounds again, cracking of branches, cries,
caterwauling, etc.*)

THE QUEEN: I thought as much. Even their botany is
wicked. Luckily we have our preserves.

THE GOVERNOR: And reserves of energy. Always fresh troops.

THE QUEEN: (*to* THE GOVERNOR). Tell them that their
sovereign is with them in her heart . . . and . . .
what about the gold? . . . the emeralds . . . the
copper . . . the mother-of-pearl?

THE MISSIONARY: (*with a finger to his mouth*). In safe places. They'll be shown to you. Pounds of them. Stacks of them. Avalanches.

THE QUEEN: (*still moving forward*). If it's at all possible, before the sun sets behind the mountains I'd like to go down to a mine and row on the lake. (*Suddenly she notices* THE VALET, *who is shivering.*) What's the matter? Scared?

THE VALET: Fever, madame.

THE QUEEN: (*shaking* THE VALET). Fever? Fever or liquor? You drank more than half the supply all by yourself.

THE VALET: I did it in order to sing better, and louder. I even danced.

THE QUEEN: (*to* THE MISSIONARY). What about the dancing? Where's the dancing?

THE MISSIONARY: It takes place only at night. . . .

THE QUEEN: Have the Night brought in!

THE GOVERNOR: It's coming, Madame! In quick time! One two! . . . One two!

(*The jungle sounds made by the* NEGROES *grow louder and louder.*)

THE MISSIONARY: (*timidly*). The dances take place only at night. Each and every one of them is danced for our destruction. Go no further. This is a dread region. Every thicket hides the grave of a missionary. . . . (*Belches.*)

THE GOVERNOR: And of a captain. (*Pointing with his arm.*) There the north, there the east, the west, the south. On each of these shores, at the river's edge, on the plains, our soldiers have fallen. Don't go any closer, it's a swamp. . . . (*He holds back* THE QUEEN.)

72

THE JUDGE: (*sternly*). The climate's no excuse for your laxity. I've lost none of my pride or daring. It was to punish a crime that I undertook the journey. Where are the Negroes, Mr. Governor?

(*The* NEGROES *laugh as before, very softly, almost in a murmur. And the same rustling of leaves, moaning of wind, roars and other sounds that suggest the virgin forest.*)

THE QUEEN: (*falling into* THE GOVERNOR'S *arms*). Did you hear? (*They all listen.*) . . . and . . . and . . . what if they were . . . if they were really Blacks? And, what if they were alive?

THE MISSIONARY: Don't be afraid, Madame. They wouldn't dare. . . . You are swathed in a gentle dawn that keeps them in awe.

THE QUEEN: (*trembling*). You think so? I haven't done anything bad, have I? Obviously, my soldiers have sometimes let themselves be carried away in their enthusiasm. . . .

THE GOVERNOR: Madame, I'm in command here, and it's not the moment to pass judgement on ourselves. . . . You're under my protection.

THE VALET: And I'm warrant of the fact that we have their welfare at heart. I've hailed their beauty in a poem that's become famous. . . .

(*The* NEGROES *have moved forward very softly. The Court stops short. Then it moves back, as softly as the* NEGROES *move forward, so that it is at the right, at the point where it entered, opposite the side where the* NEGROES *are, and facing them.*)

FELICITY: (*to the* NEGROES). It's dawn! Take it, Absalom!

ARCHIBALD: (*imitating a cock*). Cock-a-doodle-doo!

73

FELICITY: (*still addressing the* NEGROES). It's dawn, gentlemen. Since we've wanted to be guilty, let's be prepared. We must act and speak cautiously and with restraint.

THE GOVERNOR: (*to* THE VALET). I'm going to see whether there's a possibility of our falling back. (*Exit, right, but reappearing immediately.*) Madame, the jungle has closed behind us.

THE QUEEN: (*frightened*). But we're in our native land, aren't we?

THE GOVERNOR: Madame, all the shutters are closed, the dogs are hostile, communications are cut off, the night is bitter cold. It was a trap. We must make a stand. It's dawn! (*To* THE VALET.) Take it!

THE VALET: Cock-a-doodle-doo!

THE QUEEN: (*gloomily*). Yes, it's dawn, and we're face to face with them. And they're black, just as I dreamt they were.

THE JUDGE: Let's set up the court of justice!

THE MISSIONARY: (*to* THE VALET). The throne! And stop that absurd trembling. (THE VALET *brings over* FELICITY's *gilded armchair.* THE QUEEN *sits down on it.*)

(*The* NEGROES *take a step forward, then remain still.* NEWPORT NEWS *goes to the catafalque and removes the sheet, which has been stretched over two chairs.*)

THE QUEEN: My chairs!

THE VALET: They were there all the time! And I even looked for them under your skirts, Mr. Missionary!

(THE VALET *brings over the two chairs.* THE GOVERNOR *and* THE MISSIONARY *sit down on them.*

74

But first the Court bows ceremoniously to the
NEGROES *who, in like fashion, welcome the Court.*
The dolls representing the Court will remain on a
kind of pedestal at the left until the curtain is
drawn.)

DIOUF: And I who saw myself shut up in the case!

THE JUDGE: The Court is now ready. (*To* THE NEGROES.)
Lie down. You'll approach us on your bellies.

ARCHIBALD: (*to the Court*). They're worn out, sir. If we may,
we'll hear you on our haunches.

THE JUDGE: (*after exchanging glances of inquiry with the*
Court). Granted.

ARCHIBALD: (*to the* NEGROES). Squat. (*The* NEGROES *squat. To*
THE JUDGE.) May we whimper ?

THE JUDGE: If you must. (*In a booming voice.*) But first,
tremble! (*The* NEGROES *tremble in orchestrated*
fashion.) Harder! Tremble, come on, shake!
Don't be afraid to bring down the coconuts
that hang from your branches! Tremble,
Negroes! (*The* NEGROES, *all together, tremble*
harder and harder.) That'll do. . . . That'll do. . . .
We'll overlook your impertinences, which
would make us more severe. We've taken stock:
although we're not missing the body of either a
white woman or white man, God has intimated
to us that there's an extra soul on hand. What
does that mean?

ARCHIBALD: Alas, what *does* it mean?

THE MISSIONARY: (*to* THE JUDGE). Be careful. They're crafty,
artful, cunning. They're fond of trials and
theological discussions. They have a secret
telegraph that flies over hill and dale.

THE JUDGE: (*to* ARCHIBALD). I'm not accusing *all* of Africa.
That would be unjust, ungentlemanly. . . .

(THE QUEEN, THE VALET, THE MISSIONARY *and* THE
GOVERNOR *applaud*.)

THE QUEEN: Splendid! A fine and noble reply.

THE JUDGE: (*slyly*). No, one can't hold all of Africa responsible for the death of a white woman. Nevertheless, there's no denying the fact that one of
you is guilty, and we've made the journey for
the purpose of bringing him to trial. According
to our statutes—naturally. He killed out of
hatred. Hatred of the colour white. That was
tantamount to killing our entire race and
killing us till doomsday. There was no one in
the packing-case . . . tell us why.

ARCHIBALD: (*sadly*). Alas, my Lord, there was no packing-
case either.

THE GOVERNOR: No packing-case? No packing-case either?
They kill us without killing us and shut us up in
no packing-case either!

THE MISSIONARY: After that dodge, they won't be able to say they
don't fake. They've been stringing us along. (*To*
THE VALET.) Don't laugh! Don't you see what
they're doing with us?

THE JUDGE: (*to the* NEGROES). According to you, there's no
crime since there's no corpse, and no culprit
since there's no crime. But let's get things
straight: one corpse, two, a battalion, a drove
of corpses, we'll pile them high if that's what's
needed to avenge us. But no corpse at all—why
that could kill us. (*To* ARCHIBALD.) Do you
want to be the death of us?

ARCHIBALD: We are actors and organized an evening's
entertainment for you. We tried to present some
aspect of our life that might interest you.
Unfortunately, we haven't found very much.

76

THE MISSIONARY: Their dusky bodies were allowed to bear the Christian names of the Gregorian calendar. That was the first step.

THE VALET: (*insidiously*). Look at his mouth. You can see that their beauty can equal ours. Your Majesty, allow that beauty to be perpetuated. . .

THE JUDGE: For your pleasure? But my job is to seek out and judge a malefactor.

THE GOVERNOR: (*in a single breath*). And then I'll execute him: a bullet in his head and calves, spurts of saliva, Bowie knives, bayonets, pop-guns, poisons of our Medicis. . . .

THE JUDGE: He won't get out of it. I've got some tough laws, very sharp, very precise. . . .

THE GOVERNOR: Puncturing of the abdomen, adrift in the eternal snows of our unconquered glaciers, Corsican blunderbuss, brass-knuckles, the guillotine, shoelaces, the itch, epilepsy. . . .

THE JUDGE: Articles 280–8, 927–17, 18, 16, 5, 3, 2, 1, 0.

THE GOVERNOR: Tar and feathers, died like a rat, died like a dog, dyed in the wool, died in battle, hit the bottle, died in bed, cock-o'-the-walk. Hemlock. . . .

THE MISSIONARY: Gentlemen, be calm. The monster won't escape us again. But first, I'll christen him. For it's a matter of executing a man, not of bleeding an animal. And if Her Majesty. . . .

THE QUEEN: (*gently*). As usual, I'll be godmother.

THE MISSIONARY: And then I'll give absolution for his crimes. And after that, gentlemen, it'll be your turn. When it's over, we'll pray. But first, the christening.

ARCHIBALD: You're in Africa. . . .

THE QUEEN: (*ecstatically*). Overseas! Capricorn! My islands! Coral!

ARCHIBALD: (*slightly annoyed*). By being obstinate you're courting danger. Be careful. If you make one of your signs, the waters of our lakes, of our streams and rivers and cataracts, the sap of our trees and even our saliva, may boil over . . . or freeze.

THE QUEEN: In exchange for a crime, we were bringing the criminal pardon and absolution.

VILLAGE: Madame, beware. You are a great queen, and Africa is unsafe. Go back while there's still time. Go back. Withdraw.

FELICITY: (*to the* NEGROES). That'll do! Stand back! (*She makes a sign, and all the* NEGROES *withdraw to the left of the stage. Then, at a sign from* THE QUEEN, *the Court withdraws to the right. The two women are face to face.*)

THE QUEEN: (*to* FELICITY). Begin.

FELICITY: *You* begin!

THE QUEEN: (*very courteously, as one behaves with humble folk*). I assure you, I can wait. . . .

FELICITY: Admit you don't know how to begin.

THE QUEEN: I can wait. I have eternity with me.

FELICITY: (*with her hands on her hips; exploding*). Oh, really? Well, then, Dahomey! Dahomey! Negroes, back me up! And don't let the crime be glossed over. (*To* THE QUEEN.) No one could possibly deny it, it's sprouting, sprouting, my beauty, it's growing, bright and green, it's bursting into bloom, into perfume, and that lovely tree, that crime of mine, is all Africa! Birds have nested in it, and night dwells in its branches.

THE QUEEN: Every evening, and every single second, you

78

engage, against me and mine—I know you do—
in a preposterous and baleful rite. The scent of
that tree's flowers spreads all the way to my
country and tries to capture and destroy me.

FELICITY: (*face to face with* THE QUEEN). You're a ruin!

THE QUEEN: But what a ruin! And I haven't finished
sculpting myself, haven't finished carving and
jagging and fashioning myself in the form of a
ruin. An eternal ruin. It's not time that corrodes
me, it's not fatigue that makes me forsake
myself, it's death that's shaping me and that. . . .

FELICITY: If you're death itself, then why, why, do you
reproach me for killing you?

THE QUEEN: And if I'm dead, why do you go on and on
killing me, murdering me over and over in my
colour? Isn't my sublime corpse—which still
moves—enough for you? Do you need the
corpse of a corpse?

(*Side by side, almost amicably, the two women
move forward to the very front of the stage.*)

FELICITY: I shall have the corpse of your corpse's ghost.
You are pale, but you're becoming transparent.
Fog that drifts over my land, you will vanish
utterly. My sun. . . .

THE QUEEN: But if all that remained of my ghost were a
breath, and only the breath of that breath, it
would enter through the orifices of your bodies
to haunt you. . . .

FELICITY: We'd let a fart and blow you out.

THE QUEEN: (*infuriated*). Governor! General! Bishop!
Judge! Valet!

ALL: (*gloomily and without moving*). Coming.

THE QUEEN: Put them to the sword!

79

FELICITY: If you are the light and we the shade, so long as there is night into which day must sink. . . .

THE QUEEN: I'm going to have you exterminated.

FELICITY: (*ironically*). You fool, just imagine how flat you'd be without that shade to set you off in high relief.

THE QUEEN: But. . . .

FELICITY: (*same tone*). For this evening, until the end of the drama, let us therefore remain alive.

THE QUEEN: (*turning to the Court*). Good God, good God, what's one to say to her. . . .

(THE GOVERNOR, JUDGE, MISSIONARY *and* VALET *rush up to her and whisper encouragement.*)

THE MISSIONARY: Speak of our concern for them . . . of our schools. . . .

THE GOVERNOR: Bring up the white man's burden, quote some lines from Kipling. . . .

THE QUEEN: (*inspired*). All the same, my proud beauty, I was more beautiful than you! Anyone who knows me can tell you that. No one has been more lauded than I. Or more courted, or more toasted. Or adorned. Clouds of heroes, young and old, have died for me. My retinues were famous. At the Emperor's ball, an African slave bore my train. And the Southern Cross was one of my baubles. You were still in darkness. . . .

FELICITY: Beyond that shattered darkness, which was splintered into millions of Blacks who dropped to the jungle, we were Darkness in person. Not the darkness which is absence of light, but the kindly and terrible Mother who contains light and deeds.

80

THE QUEEN: (*as if in a panic, to the Court*). Well? What else. . . .

THE GOVERNOR: Say that we have guns to silence them. . . .

THE MISSIONARY: That's idiotic. No, be friendly. . . . Mention Dr. Livingstone. . . .

FELICITY: Behold our gestures. Though now they're merely the mutilated arms of our ravaged rites, bogged down in weariness and time, before long you'll be stretching lopped-off stumps to heaven and to us. . . .

THE QUEEN: (*to the Court*). What should I answer?

FELICITY: Look! Look, Madame. Here it comes, the darkness you were clamouring for, and her sons as well. They're her escort of crimes. To you, black was the colour of priests and undertakers and orphans. But everything is changing. Whatever is gentle and kind and good and tender will be black. Milk will be black, sugar, rice, the sky, doves, hope, will be black. So will the opera to which we shall go, blacks that we are, in black Rolls Royces to hail black kings, to hear brass bands, beneath chandeliers of black crystal. . . .

THE QUEEN: But, after all, I haven't said my last word. . . .

THE VALET: (*in her ear*). Sing a psalm!

THE MISSIONARY: Can't be helped—show your legs!

FELICITY: Twelve hours of night. Our merciful mother will keep us in her house, huddled between her walls! Twelve hours of day, so that these fragments of darkness can perform for the sun ceremonies like those of this evening. . . .

THE QUEEN: (*very upset*). You fool! You see only the beauty of history. It's all well and good to come

81

insulting us beneath our windows and to give
birth every day to a hundred new heroes who
put on an act. . . .

FELICITY: Before long you'll see what's hidden behind
our display. . . . You're exhausted, all of you. . . .
Your journey has worn you out. You're
dropping with sleep. . . . You're dreaming!

THE QUEEN: (*she and* FELICITY *now talk to each other like two
women exchanging recipes*). Yes, that's so. But
what about you? You're going to tire yourselves
too. And don't expect me to suggest tonics.
Your herbs won't do the trick.

FELICITY: I don't mind being dog-tired. Others will help
me.

THE QUEEN: And what about your darkies? Your slaves?
Where will you get them? . . . You'll need
them, you know. . . .

FELICITY: (*timidly*). You might, perhaps. . . . We'll be
good negroes. . . .

THE QUEEN: Oh no, not on your life! Governesses? Well,
maybe. . . .

THE MISSIONARY: If absolutely necessary, tutors for children . . .
and even then. . . .

FELICITY: It'll be hard, won't it?

THE QUEEN: (*leading her on*). Awful. But you'll be strong.
And we, we'll be charmers. We'll be lascivious.
We'll dance in order to be seductive. Just
imagine what you're in for. Long labour on
continents, for centuries, to carve yourself a
sepulchre that may be less beautiful than
mine. . . . So let me manage things, won't you?
No? You see how tired you are already. What
is it you want? No, no, don't answer. Is it that

you want your sons to be free of chains? Is that it? That's a noble wish, but listen to me . . . follow me . . . your sons—why, you don't know them yet. . . . You do? Their feet are already riveted together? Your grandsons? They're unborn: so they don't exist. Therefore you can't worry about their situation. What does freedom or slavery matter since they don't exist? Really . . . smile a little! . . . Really, my argument seems false? (*The* NEGROES *all look gloomy.*) Come, come, gentlemen. (*Addressing her retinue.*) Can I be wrong?

THE MISSIONARY: You are wisdom itself.

THE QUEEN: (*to* FELICITY). Your grandsons—who, bear in mind, do not exist—will have nothing to do. They'll serve us, no doubt, but we're not demanding. But think of the hardships for *us*. We'll have to *be*. And be radiant. (*A silence.*)

FELICITY: (*gently*). And you, think of the mosquitoes of our swamps. If they stung me, a grown Negro, fully armed, would spring from each abscess. . . .

THE MISSIONARY: (*to* THE QUEEN). Madame, I told you so. They're insolent, bitter, vindictive. . . .

THE QUEEN: (*weeping*). But what have I done to them? I'm kind, and sweet, and beautiful!

THE MISSIONARY: (*to the* NEGROES). You nasty things! Look at the state into which you've dared to put the kindest, sweetest and most beautiful of women!

SNOW: The most beautiful?

THE MISSIONARY: (*embarrassed*). I meant the most beautiful in our country. Display a little good will. Look at how she got all dressed up to visit you, and think of all we've done for you. We've baptized you! All of you! What about the water it took to baptize you? And the salt? The salt on your tongues. Tons of salt painfully extracted from mines. But here I am going on and on and in a moment I'll have to allow his Excellency the Governor to speak, and he'll be followed by His Lordship the Judge. Why be massacred instead of recognizing. . . .

THE JUDGE: Who's the culprit? (*Silence.*) You won't answer? I'm offering you one last chance. Now listen: it doesn't matter to us which of you committed the crime. We don't care whether it's X, Y or Z. If a man's a man, a negro's a negro, and all we need is two arms, two legs to break, a neck to put into the noose, and our justice is satisfied. Come, be decent about it.

(*Suddenly a firecracker explodes off-stage, followed by several more. The sparks of fireworks are seen against the black velvet of the set. Finally, everything grows quiet. The* NEGROES, *who were squatting behind* FELICITY, *stand up.*)

NEWPORT NEWS: (*stepping forth*). I wish to inform you. . . .

(*With a single movement, the members of the Court solemnly remove their masks. The audience sees the five black faces.*)

VILLAGE: (*very anxiously*). Is he dead?

NEWPORT NEWS: He has paid. We shall have to get used to the responsibility of executing our own traitors.

THE ONE WHO PLAYED THE VALET: (*sternly*). Did everything go off with all due justice?

NEWPORT NEWS: (*deferentially*). Rest assured. Not only were the forms of justice applied, but the spirit as well.

THE ONE WHO PLAYED THE MISSIONARY: What about the defence?

NEWPORT NEWS: Perfect. Very eloquent. But it was unable to

sway the jury. And execution followed almost immediately upon delivery of sentence.

(*A silence.*)

THE ONE WHO PLAYED THE QUEEN: And now?

NEWPORT NEWS: Now? While a court was sentencing the one who was just executed, a congress was acclaiming another. He's on his way. He's going off to organize and continue the fight. Our aim is not only to corrode and dissolve the idea they'd like us to have of them, we must also fight them in their actual persons, in their flesh and blood. As for you, you were present only for display. Behind. . . .

THE ONE WHO PLAYED THE VALET: (*curtly*). We know. Thanks to us, they've sensed nothing of what's going on elsewhere.

(*A silence.*)

THE ONE WHO PLAYED THE QUEEN: And . . . you say he has already left?

NEWPORT NEWS: That's right. Everything was planned for his departure.

THE ONE WHO PLAYED THE QUEEN: And . . . what is he like?

NEWPORT NEWS: (*smiling*). Just as you imagine him. Exactly as he must be in order to spread panic by force and cunning.

ALL: (*speaking at the same time*). Describe him! . . . Show us parts of him! . . . Let's see his knee, his calf, his toe! . . . His eye! His teeth!

NEWPORT NEWS: (*laughing*). He's on his way. Let him go. He has our confidence. Everything has been planned and prepared so that he can count on us when he's away.

85

THE ONE WHO PLAYED THE GOVERNOR: What about his voice? What's his voice like?

NEWPORT NEWS: It's deep. Somewhat caressing. He'll first have to fascinate and then convince. Yes, he's also a charmer.

BOBO: (*suspiciously*). But . . . at least he's black?

(*For a moment, they are all puzzled; then they burst out laughing.*)

THE ONE WHO PLAYED THE MISSIONARY: We've got to hurry. . . .

VILLAGE: Are you leaving?

THE ONE WHO PLAYED THE GOVERNOR: Everything has been planned for each of us. If we want to get things done, we haven't a minute to lose.

DIOUF: I. . . .

THE ONE WHO PLAYED THE MISSIONARY: (*interrupting him very brusquely*). It'll be hard for the others too—especially in the early stages—to shake off the torpor of a whole continent. Hemmed in by vapours and flies, imprisoned in pollen. . . .

DIOUF: (*whimpering*). I'm old. . . . I may be forgotten . . . and, besides they draped me in such a pretty dress. . . .

THE ONE WHO PLAYED THE VALET: (*sternly*). Keep it. If they've turned you into the image they want to have of us, then stay with them. You'd be a burden to us.

ARCHIBALD: (*to* THE ONE WHO PLAYED THE VALET). But—is he still acting or is he speaking for himself? (*Hesitating.*) An Actor . . . a Negro . . . who wants to kill turns even his knife into something make-believe. (*To* DIOUF.) Are you staying? (*A brief silence.* DIOUF *bows his head.*) Then stay.

86

SNOW: I've got to be going.

THE ONE WHO PLAYED THE VALET: Not before we finish the performance. (*To* ARCHIBALD.) Resume the tone.

ARCHIBALD: (*solemnly*). As we could not allow the Whites to be present at a deliberation nor show them a drama that does not concern them, and as, in order to cover up, we have had to fabricate the only one that does concern them, we've got to finish this show and get rid of our judges . . . (*to* THE ONE WHO PLAYED THE QUEEN) as planned.

THE ONE WHO PLAYED THE QUEEN: At last they'll know the only dramatic relationships we can have with them. (*To the four* NEGROES *of the Court.*) Are you willing?

THE ONE WHO PLAYED THE JUDGE: We are.

THE ONE WHO PLAYED THE QUEEN: We masked our faces in order to live the loathsome life of the Whites and at the same time to help you sink into shame, but our roles as actors are drawing to a close.

ARCHIBALD: How far are you willing to go?

THE ONE WHO PLAYED THE GOVERNOR: To the bitter end.

VILLAGE: But . . . except for the flowers, we haven't provided anything . . . neither knives nor guns nor gallows nor rivers nor bayonets. Will we have to slit your throats in order to get rid of you?

THE ONE WHO PLAYED THE QUEEN: There's no need to. We're actors, our massacre will be lyrical. (*To the four* NEGROES *of the Court.*) Gentlemen, your masks. (*One after the other, they put on their masks again.*) (*To* ARCHIBALD.) As for you, all you need to do is give us our cues. All set?

ARCHIBALD: Begin.

87

THE QUEEN: You may start, Mr. Governor.

FELICITY: But, Madame, we haven't finished our oratorical contest. Don't deprive me of the best part. There's still lots to be said against Negroes.

THE QUEEN: I have made the journey. It was a long one. Your warmth is inhuman, and I prefer to depart. . . .

FELICITY: Nevertheless, you're going to hear what the colour white will signify from now on.

THE QUEEN: Don't waste your time. We'll be off and away before you've even finished your speech.

FELICITY: If we let you leave.

THE QUEEN: How simple-minded! You haven't realized that we're heading for death. We're going to it voluntarily, with a sneaking happiness.

FELICITY: Are you committing suicide? You? (*All the* NEGROES *and the members of the Court, except* THE QUEEN, *burst into loud, free laughter.*)

THE QUEEN: We choose to die so as to deprive you of pride of triumph. Unless you're going to boast of having conquered a people of shadows.

FELICITY: We'll always be able. . . .

THE QUEEN: (*with great authority*). Be quiet. It's for me to speak and to give my orders. (*To* THE GOVERNOR.) As I said, you may begin, Mr. Governor.

THE GOVERNOR: People usually draw lots in such circumstances. . . .

THE QUEEN: No explanations. Show these barbarians that we are great because of our respect for discipline, and show the Whites who are watching that we are worthy of their tears.

ARCHIBALD: No. No, please don't die. Mr. Governor, please
stay! What we enjoyed was to kill you, to
slaughter you down to your white powder, to
your very soapsuds. . . .

THE QUEEN: Ah, ah! I've got you. (*To* THE GOVERNOR.)
Governor, lead off!

THE GOVERNOR: (*with resignation*). Very well! Colonially
speaking, I've served my country well. (*He
takes a swig of rum.*) I've been given a
thousand nicknames, which proved the Queen's
esteem and the savage's fear. So I'm going to
die, but in an apotheosis, borne aloft by ten
thousand lads leaner than Plague and Leprosy,
exalted by anger and fury. (*At this point,* THE
GOVERNOR *takes a paper from his pocket, as he
did at the beginning of the play, and reads.*)
When I fall to earth, scurvily pierced by your
spears, look closely, you will behold my
ascension. My corpse will be on the ground, but
my soul and body will rise into the air. You'll
see them, and you'll die of fright. It is thus that
I have chosen to conquer you and rid the earth
of your shadows. First, you'll turn pale, then
you'll fall, and you'll be dead. And I, great. (*He
puts the paper back into his pocket.*) Sublime.
Terrifying. (*Silence.*) Well, you won't speak?
What? You say I'm trembling? You know very
well it's military gout. (*Silence.*) Well, you won't
speak? Oh, you're resentful because of the ten
thousand lads who were crushed by my tanks?
After all, can't a warrior make growing boys
bite the dust? . . . (*He trembles more and more
violently.*) No, I'm not trembling more and more
violently, I'm sending alarm signals to my
troops. . . . All the same, you're not going to
kill me for good? . . . You are? . . . You're
not? . . . Well, all right, take aim at this

89

indomitable heart. I die childless . . . but I'm counting on your sense of honour to donate my bloodstained uniform to the Army Museum. Ready, aim, fire!

(VILLAGE *points a revolver and shoots, but there is no sound of a shot.* THE GOVERNOR *falls.*)

ARCHIBALD: (*indicating the middle of the stage*). No. Come and die here. (*With his heel,* ARCHIBALD *sets off a small cap, the kind children play with.* THE GOVERNOR, *who has stood up, goes to the middle of the stage and falls there.*)

THE GOVERNOR: My liver bursting, my heart bleeding.

THE NEGROES: (*bursting into laughter and, in chorus, imitating the crowing of a cock*). Cock-a-doodle-doo!

ARCHIBALD: Off to Hell. (*To* THE QUEEN.) Next.

(VILLAGE *and* VIRTUE *have stepped away from the group of* NEGROES *and come to the front of the stage, left.* VIRTUE *pretends to be flirting.*)

VILLAGE: When I come back, I'll bring you perfumes. . .

VIRTUE: And what else?

VILLAGE: Wild strawberries.

VIRTUE: You're silly. And who'll pick the strawberries? You? Squatting and looking for them under the leaves. . . .

VILLAGE: I'm doing it to please you, and you. . . .

VIRTUE: My pride? I want you to bring me. . . .

(*They continue flirting during* THE JUDGE'S *speech.*)

THE JUDGE: (*standing up*). I understand. I won't use eloquence. I know all too well what that leads to. No, I've drafted a bill, the first paragraph c

90

which reads as follows: Act of July 18th. Article 1. God being dead, the colour black ceases to be a sin; it becomes a crime. . . .

ARCHIBALD: You'll have your head sliced off, but sliced into slices.

THE JUDGE: You have no right. . . . (*A shot is heard.*)

ARCHIBALD: Off to Hell!

(*Slowly* THE JUDGE *falls upon* THE GOVERNOR. *The moment he falls,* THE NEGROES *cry out in chorus.*)

THE NEGROES: Cock-a-doodle-doo!

ARCHIBALD: Next.

VIRTUE: (*to* VILLAGE; *both of them are now at the extreme left of the stage.*) I, too, for a long time didn't dare love you. . . .

VILLAGE: You love me?

VIRTUE: I would listen. I would hear you striding along· I would run to the window and from behind the curtain would watch you go by. . . .

VILLAGE: (*bantering tenderly*). You were wasting your time. I strolled by like an indifferent male, without a glance . . . but at night I would come and capture a beam of light from between your shutters. I would carry it off between my shirt and skin.

VIRTUE: And I, I was already in bed, with your image. Other girls may guard the image of their beloved in their hearts or eyes. Yours was between my teeth. I would bite into it. . . .

VILLAGE: In the morning, I would proudly display the marks of your bites.

91

VIRTUE: (*putting her hand over his mouth*). Be still.

THE MISSIONARY: (*standing up*). It was I who brought you
knowledge of Hell. How dare you cast me
into it? Why, that's preposterous. Hell obeys
me. It opens or closes at a sign from my ringed
hand. I have blessed brides and grooms,
christened piccaninnies, ordained battalions of
black priests, and I brought you the message of
One Who was crucified. I understand you—for
if the Church speaks all languages, she likewise
understands them all—you reproach Christ for
his colour. Let us bear in mind that no sooner
was He born than a black prince, who was a bit
of a sorcerer, came to adore Him. . . .
(*Suddenly, he breaks off. He looks at the
motionless* NEGROES. *He is visibly frightened.
Panicky.*) No, no! Gentlemen, gentlemen, don't
do that! (*He trembles more and more violently.*)
Ladies, ladies, I beg of you! It would be too
awful! In the name of the Heavenly Virgin,
appeal to your husbands, your brothers, your
lovers! Gentlemen, gentlemen, no, no, not that!
In the first place, I don't believe in it. No, I
don't believe in it. Hell, which I brought to you.
. . . I've mistreated your sorcerers—oh, I'm
sorry! Not your sorcerers, gentlemen, your
miracle-workers, your priests, your clergy. . . .
I've made jokes, I've blasphemed, I should be
punished, but not that! . . . Gentlemen, gentlemen, I beg of you. . . . Don't make the gesture.
. . . don't utter the formula. . . . No, no. . . .
(*The* NEGROES *become more and more frozen, set,
impassive. All at once,* THE MISSIONARY *becomes
calm. He no longer trembles. He breathes more
easily. He seems relieved, almost smiling;
suddenly he blurts out.*) Moo! . . . Moo! . . .
(*Still mooing like a cow, he walks about on all*

fours, *pretends to graze, and licks the feet of the* NEGROES, *who have stepped back, as if somewhat frightened.*)

ARCHIBALD: That'll do. To the slaughterhouse.

(THE MISSIONARY *gets up and goes to fall on* THE GOVERNOR *and* JUDGE.)

THE MISSIONARY: (*screaming in a falsetto voice before falling*). Castrated! I've been castrated! I'll be canonized, high, stiff and firm.

ARCHIBALD: Next!

THE VALET: (*standing up and trembling*). Are you going to beat me? I can't stand physical pain, you know, for I was the artist. In a way, I was one of you, I too was a victim of the Governor General and the established authorities. You say that I revered them? Yes and no. I was very disrespectful. You fascinated me far more than they did. In any case, this evening I'm no longer what I was yesterday, for I also know how to betray. If you like, though without quite going over to your side . . . I can. . . .

THE QUEEN: (*to* THE VALET). At least say to them that without us their revolt would be meaningless— wouldn't even exist. . . .

THE VALET: (*still trembling*). They refuse to hear anything more. (*To the* NEGROES.) I'll bring you trade secrets, plans. . . .

(*The* NEGROES *clap their hands and stamp their feet as if to frighten him.* THE VALET *runs away and falls on the heap formed by* THE GOVERNOR, MISSIONARY *and* JUDGE. *Orchestrated laughter of the* NEGROES.)

ARCHIBALD: Off to Hell!

THE QUEEN: (*standing up solemnly*). Well, are you satisfied? Now I am alone. (*A shot.*) And dead. Beheaded, like my illustrious cousin. I too shall take with me my flock of corpses that you keep killing so that they may stay alive and that you keep alive in order to kill. But, be well assured, we had become unworthy only of you. It was easy for you to transform us into an allegory, but I had to live and suffer in order to become that image . . . and I have even loved . . . loved (*suddenly she changes her tone and, turning to* ARCHIBALD) but, tell me, sir, that negro (*she points to* DIOUF) who served you as a prop for killing a corpse, and since it's customary, once they're dead, for those corpses to rise to Heaven and judge us. . . .

SNOW: (*laughing*). And hurry down to Hell again!

THE QUEEN: I grant you that, young lady, but tell me at least, before I die, what has that one become in our Court? With what title have you adorned him, with what hatred have you charged him? What image has he become, what symbol?

(*They are all attentive; even the dead characters heaped on the ground raise their heads to listen.*)

THE GOVERNOR: (*lying on the ground*). Yes, who? What other prince? (*The* NEGROES *seem rather puzzled.*)

DIOUF: (*very gently*). Don't mind me, Mr. Archibald. I've reached the point where I can hear anything.

ARCHIBALD: (*after a silence*). The collection would have been incomplete without the Mother. (*To* DIOUF.) Tomorrow, and in the ceremonies to come, you'll represent the Worthy Mother of the heroes who died thinking they'd killed us, but

94

who were devoured by our fury and our black ants.

(*The characters lying on the ground stand up and bow to* DIOUF, *who returns their bow. Then they lie down again in a heap, as if dead.*)

DIOUF: (*to the Dead*). Well then, I'm coming down to bury you, since that's indicated in the script. (*He leaves the balcony.*)

THE QUEEN: (*to* ARCHIBALD, *admiringly*). How well you hate! (*A pause.*) How I have loved! And now, I die—I must confess—choked by my desire for a Big Black Buck. Black nakedness, thou hast conquered me.

SNOW: (*gently*). You've got to go, Madame. You're losing all your blood, and the stairway to death is interminable. And bright as day. Pale. White. Infernal.

THE QUEEN: (*to her Court*). On your feet! (*All four stand up.*) Come with me to Hell. And mind your P's and Q's when we get there. (*She pushes them along like a flock.*)

ARCHIBALD: (*stopping her*). Just a moment. The performance is coming to an end and you're about to disappear. My friends, allow me first to thank you all. You've given an excellent performance. (*The five members of the Court remove their masks and bow.*) You've displayed a great deal of courage, but you had to. The time has not yet come for presenting dramas about noble matters. But perhaps they suspect what lies behind this architecture of emptiness and words. We are what they want us to be. We shall therefore be it to the very end, absurdly. Put your masks on again before leaving. Have them escorted to Hell.

(The five characters put their masks on.)

THE QUEEN: *(turning to the* NEGROES). Farewell, and good luck to you. Young lady, I hope all goes well with you. As for us, we've lived a long time. We're now going to rest at last. (FELICITY *makes a gesture of impatience.)* We're going, we're going, but keep in mind that we shall lie torpid in the earth like larvae or moles, and if some day . . . ten thousand years hence. . . .

(Exeunt right, while the NEGROES, *except* VIRTUE *and* VILLAGE, *leave quietly, left.* VILLAGE *and* VIRTUE *remain alone on the stage. They seem to be arguing.)*

VILLAGE: But if I take your hands in mine? If I put my arms around your shoulders—let me—if I hug you?

VIRTUE: All men are like you: they imitate. Can't you invent something else?

VILLAGE: For you I could invent anything: fruits, brighter words, a two-wheeled wheelbarrow, cherries without pits, a bed for three, a needle that doesn't prick. But gestures of love, that's harder . . . still, if you really want me to. . . .

VIRTUE: I'll help you. At least, there's one sure thing: you won't be able to wind your fingers in my long golden hair. . . .

(The black backdrop rises. All the NEGROES— *including those who constituted the Court and who are without their masks—are standing about a white-draped catafalque like the one seen at the beginning of the play. Opening measures of the minuet from* Don Giovanni. *Hand in hand,* VILLAGE *and* VIRTUE *walk toward them, thus turning their backs to the audience. The curtain is drawn.)*

THE END